MURALS of NORTH NASHVILLE NOW

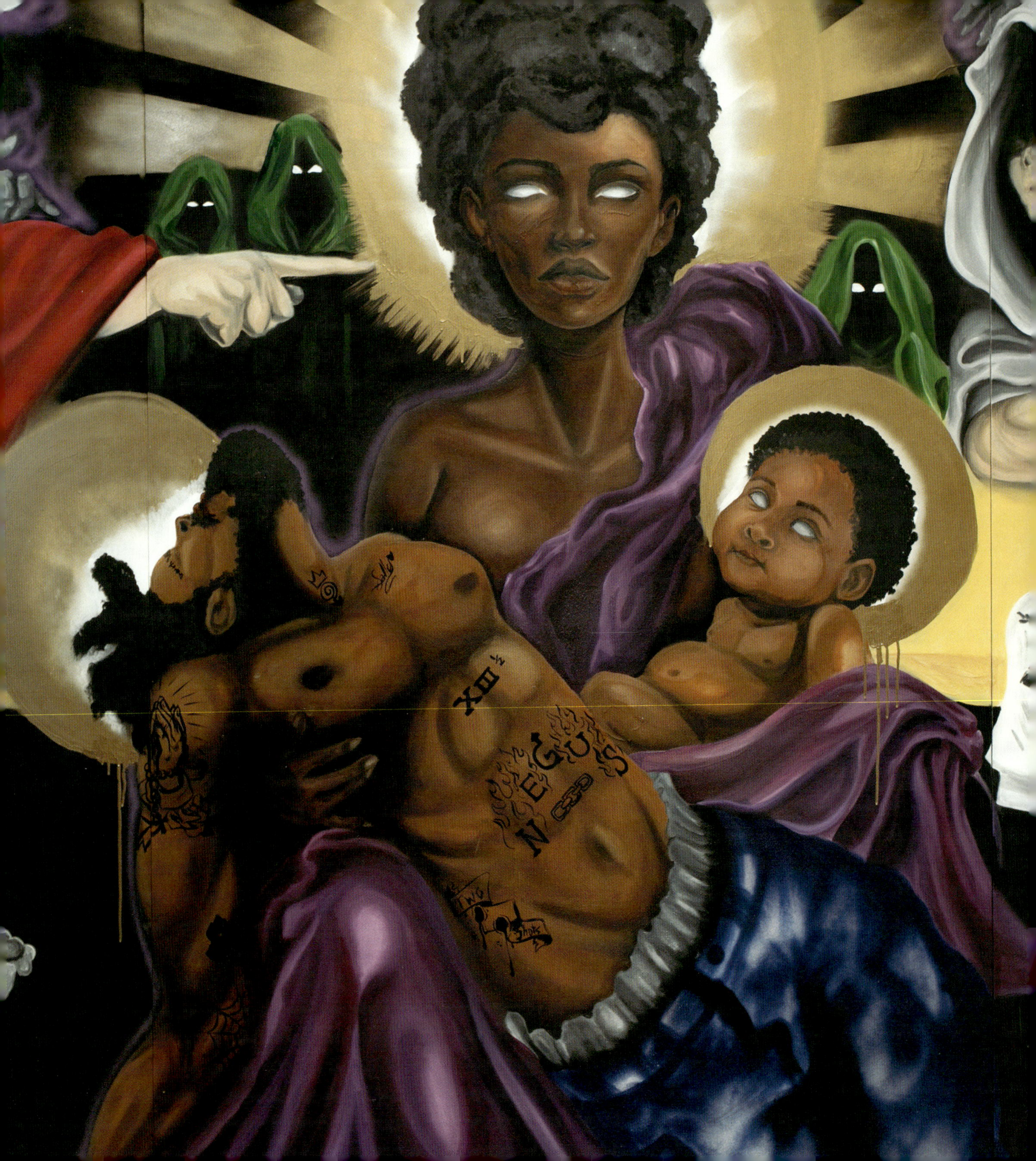
NEGUS

MURALS of NORTH NASHVILLE NOW

EDITED BY
Kathryn E. Delmez

CONTRIBUTORS
Kathryn E. Delmez
Susan H. Edwards
Learotha Williams Jr.

Frist Art Museum in association with
Vanderbilt University Press
Nashville, Tennessee

© 2019 Frist Art Museum

Published by the Frist Art Museum
and Vanderbilt University Press

Library of Congress Control
Number: 2019952023
ISBN 978-0-8265-2284-9

All rights reserved. No part of this publication may be reproduced, stored in a retrieval system, or transmitted in any form or by any means, electronic, mechanical, photocopying, recording, or otherwise, without permission in writing from the publisher.

Frist Art Museum
Philip M. El Rassi, graphic design
Wallace Joiner, managing editor

Vanderbilt University Press
Joell Smith-Borne, managing production editor
Zachary Gresham, editor

COVER: Brandon Donahue. *Rest in Peace*, 2019. Courtesy of the artist. © Brandon Donahue

BACK COVER: Norf Art Collective. *Forever*, 2019. Courtesy of the artists. © Norf Art Collective

Published in conjunction with the exhibition *Murals of North Nashville Now*, August 10, 2019–January 5, 2020, at the Frist Art Museum, Nashville, Tennessee

Curator
Kathryn E. Delmez

Exhibition design
Hans Schmitt-Matzen

Graphic design
Philip M. El Rassi

Organized by

Frist Art Museum

Presenting sponsor

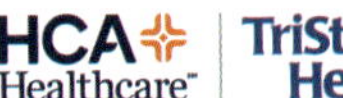

All photography of the exhibition objects and artists were taken by LeXander Bryant unless otherwise noted.

Supported in part by our **O'Keeffe Circle members** and

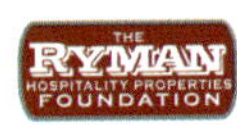

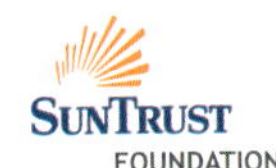

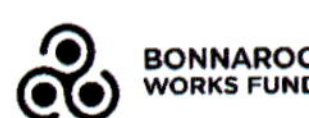

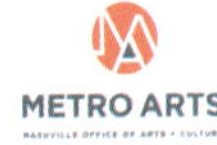

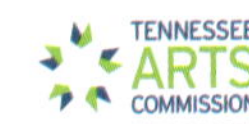

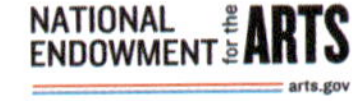

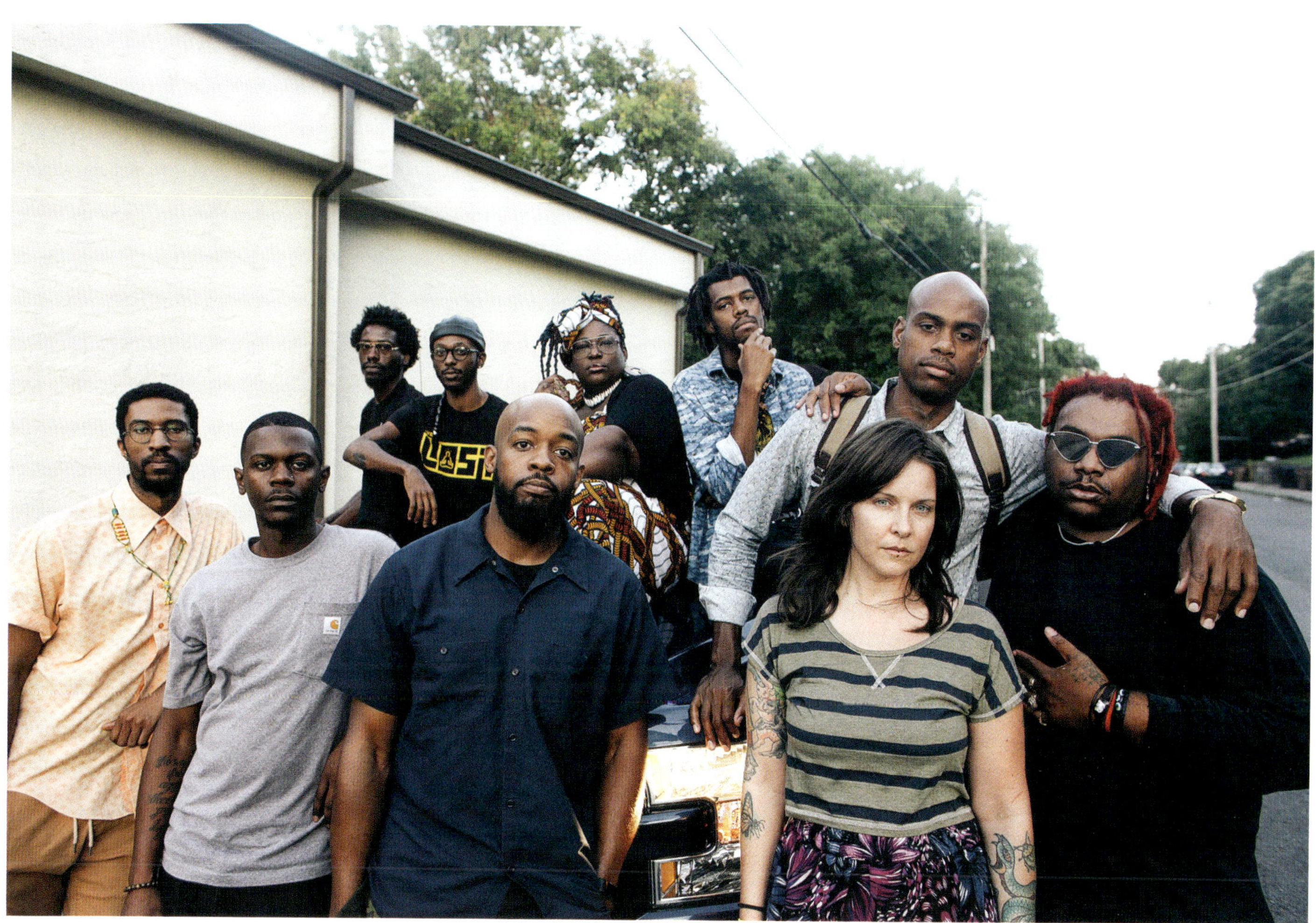

Exhibition artists. Photo: Kept Frozen

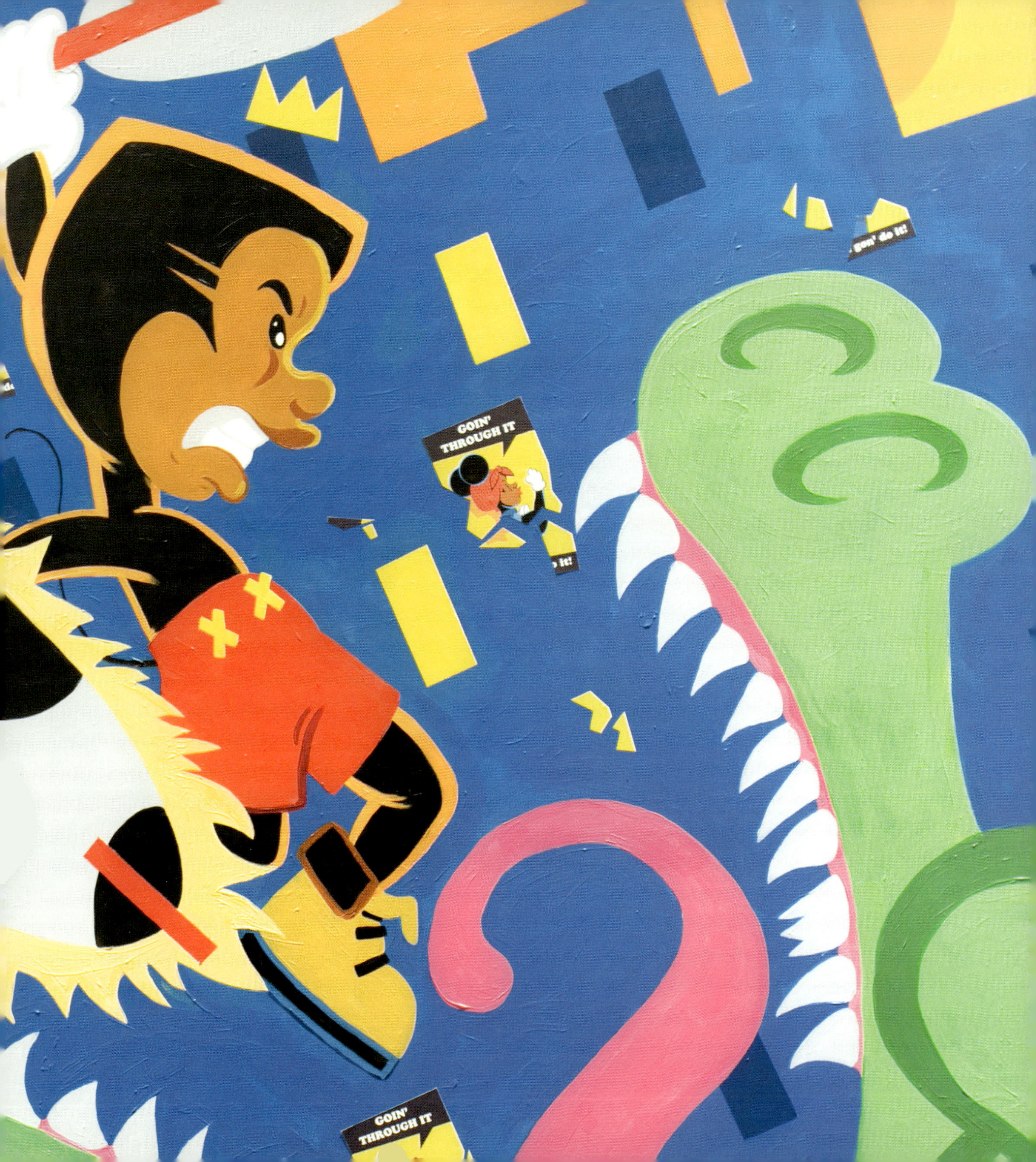
GOIN' THROUGH IT
GOIN' THROUGH IT

CONTENTS

Foreword and Acknowledgments 1
Susan H. Edwards

Introduction 5
Kathryn E. Delmez

A Balm in Gilead: Love, Hope, and Despair in North Nashville 11
Learotha Williams Jr.

Artist Entries 25
Kathryn E. Delmez

Contributors 55

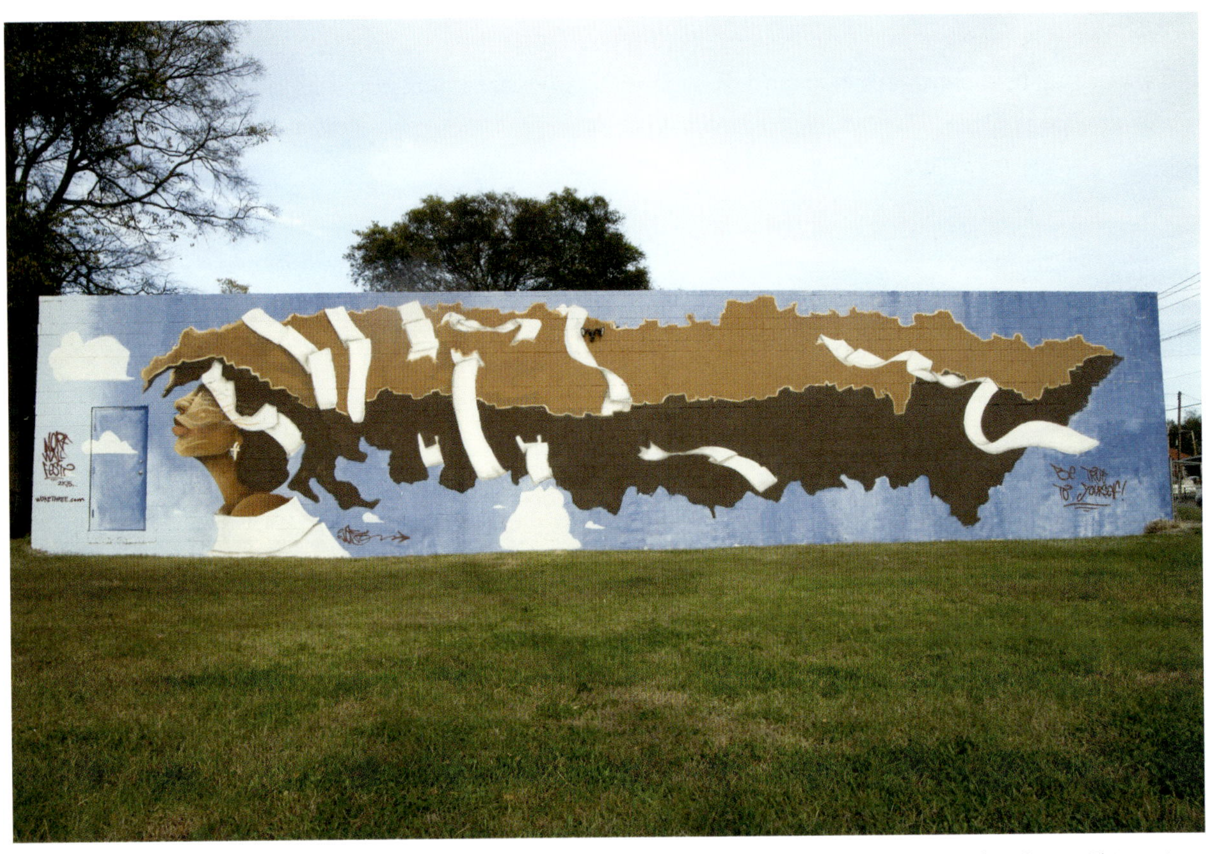

Woke3. *Breeze*, 2015. Located at 1114 Buchanan Street (buffed, no longer visible). Created for the Norf Wall Fest. This project was funded in part by the Metro Arts THRIVE program. © Woke3. Photo: keep3

FOREWORD AND ACKNOWLEDGMENTS

From cave paintings, ancient and Renaissance frescoes, and murals created during the 1930s to the current era, artists have made marks, stenciled images, etched, and painted on interior and exterior walls. Much of our knowledge of history has come to us through the depiction of everyday activities, religious traditions, social and political commentaries, and the changing standards of beauty found in murals. In the timely and provocative exhibition *Murals of North Nashville Now*, we see how area mural artists respond to local history and topical concerns. This companion book documents the 2019 exhibition held in the Conte Community Arts Gallery at the Frist Art Museum and offers insight into the context of North Nashville as well as the artists' strategies and intentions.

The Frist Art Museum (originally the Frist Center for the Visual Arts) opened in 2001. Housed in the former main post office, the 1934 structure was repurposed for a different democratic use while retaining its status on the National Register of Historic Places. Coincidentally, in the 1930s and 1940s murals were created for post offices across the country by artists working for the Works Progress Administration (WPA). In addition to providing jobs for the artists, the mural projects were designed to be accessible to all people and to boost the morale of those suffering from the effects of the Great Depression. Exhibitions in the Conte Community Arts Gallery feature art, artists, and issues of concern in Nashville. Admission to this gallery is free to all.

Curator Kathryn Delmez points out in her introduction that renowned artist Aaron Douglas was commissioned in 1930 to produce a series of murals for the Cravath Library (now Cravath Hall) at Fisk University, establishing the mural tradition in North Nashville. Michael McBride, James Threalkill, Sam Dunson, and Michael "Ol Skool" Mucker brought the practice into the twenty-first century with their own projects. The Norf Wall Fest in 2015, conceived by Tennessee State University graduate Jay Jenkins (Woke3), sparked a renaissance in the area, and murals have subsequently appeared along Jefferson Street, Buchanan Street, Clarksville Pike, under Jubilee Bridge, and in commercial spaces such as Slim & Husky's Pizza Beeria.

Recent murals in North Nashville are unified by their ability to address social issues and speak with power and conviction to the ethos of the rapidly changing neighborhood. It is not an exaggeration to claim that the artists responsible for the North Nashville murals and who participated in the Frist exhibition have reframed assumptions about their neighborhood by creating a platform for civic discourse.

There is no substitute for seeing large-scale murals in situ. Still, we are deeply honored that artists responded to Delmez's invitation to produce new works for display at the Frist that inspire viewers to see and study the murals in both settings. We are deeply indebted to the artists participating in *Murals of North Nashville Now*: Norf Art Collective (doughjoe, keep3, Sensei, and Woke3), Omari Booker, LeXander Bryant, Brandon Donahue, Elisheba Israel Mrozik, and XPayne. In addition, Nuveen Barwari, Marlos E'van, and Courtney Adair Johnson worked with youth from Oasis Center and the Opportunity NOW internship program at the McGruder Family Resource Center to create an additional mural to be exhibited in the Conte Community Arts Gallery.

Delmez often described the project as collaborative and a forum for many voices and various perspectives on art and engagement. The artists were forthcoming with their time, and we thank them for their professionalism, enthusiasm, and cooperation throughout the organization of the exhibition. Special thanks are due to Woke3 and Brandon Donahue for their wise counsel during the early stages of planning. Interns Isabelle Sagraves and Allie Blankenship assisted with preliminary research and attended to myriad details. Frist educators for community engagement Rosemary Brunton and Shaun Giles coordinated the McGruder mural. They worked closely with Frist teaching assistant Kelsey Kile and Opportunity NOW apprentice Michayla George. Youth participants were at the heart of the McGruder mural, and we have been inspired and encouraged by their creativity and good humor. Our colleagues at the McGruder Family Resource Center; Oasis Center, especially Mitchell Morrison, Hannah Beath, and Carmen Nelson; Fisk University Galleries; and Lorenzo Washington at Jefferson Street Sound warrant recognition and heartfelt gratitude. As always, we are indebted to our Frist Art Museum colleagues for their reliable and consummate professionalism in bringing the exhibition to fruition.

We thank Learotha Williams Jr., associate professor of African American and public history at Tennessee State University, who runs the North Nashville Heritage Project, for his essay explaining the past and setting the stage for the current burgeoning of mural art in the community. The exhibition schedule at the Frist Art Museum is enriched by the scholarly interests of Kathryn Delmez. Her roles in the project as curator, essayist, and editor of this volume exemplify her tireless commitment to art as a bridge to greater empathy and understanding. We are better informed and more compassionate observers and citizens because of her. For the production of this publication, we thank Frist graphic designer Phil El Rassi for a complementary and dynamic design and editor Peg Duthie, whose attention to detail goes hand in hand with a genuine understanding of content and import. Frist managing editor Wallace Joiner shepherded production through channels internally while serving with standard aplomb and efficiency as liaison with Vanderbilt University Press. At Vanderbilt, we gratefully acknowledge the support of director Gianna Mosser, who fully embraces the significance of documenting for posterity this landmark exhibition. On behalf of all of us involved in this project, we thank Zack Gresham, acquisitions editor, and production manager Joell Smith-Borne.

Murals of North Nashville Now was funded by generous grants from HCA/TriStar Health, Ryman Hospitality Properties Foundation, Bonnaroo Works Fund, and SunTrust Foundation. The Frist Art Museum gratefully acknowledges additional contributions provided by our O'Keeffe Circle members. For general operating support, we thank our colleagues and the leadership of the Metro Nashville Arts Commission, the Tennessee Arts Commission, and the National Endowment for the Arts. We are grateful to the Frist Art Museum Board of Trustees, especially Billy Frist, president and chair, for abiding faith and endorsement.

North Nashville murals and those in our exhibition have inspired conversations at the Frist Art Museum and elsewhere about displacement, disparity, urban renewal, rebirth, and optimism. Being better informed about the living and working conditions of the entire community can only lead to our being more compassionate neighbors. We are pleased to offer this publication as a lasting document of a shining moment in the history of North Nashville as seen through the eyes and art of its mural artists.

Susan H. Edwards, PhD

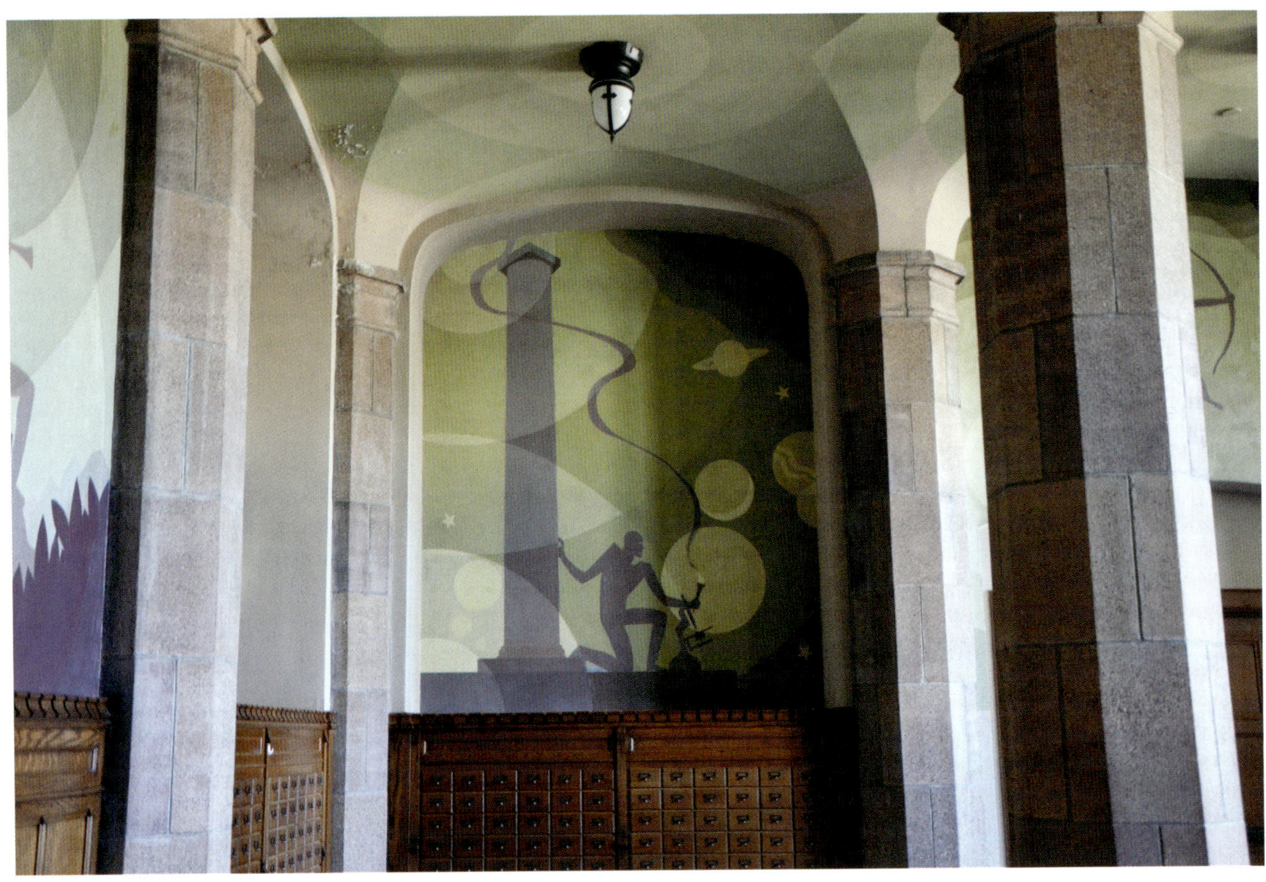

Figure 1
Aaron Douglas. One of several murals commissioned by Fisk University for the card catalog room in the Cravath Library (now Cravath Hall), 1930. Photo: Wallace Joiner

INTRODUCTION

In 2018, the historically African American neighborhood of North Nashville was featured twice on the cover of the *Nashville Scene*, an alternative weekly publication. One article lauded the "magic on Jefferson Street" that surrounded thriving cultural and artist-led initiatives, including the Student Ambassador Program at Fisk University's Carl Van Vechten Gallery, the Jefferson Street Art Crawl, and Thaxton Waters's Art History Class Lifestyle Lounge & Gallery.[1] It also pointed to successful black-owned businesses such as Woodcuts Gallery & Framing and One Drop Ink Tattoo Parlour, which serve as vital artistic hubs in addition to their primary operations. Restaurants like The Garden Brunch Café, The Southern V, and Slim & Husky's Pizza Beeria (which is rapidly expanding to Atlanta, Chattanooga, Memphis, and other areas) are offering both high-quality food and convenient jobs to the community. The other *Scene* piece reported on the area's history of displacement, from 1968, when the construction of Interstate 40 literally destroyed dozens of homes and business and left the neighborhood permanently bisected, to the present day, as gentrification pushes out many longtime residents.[2] That article also discussed a national study whose authors found that 37208—a zip code that encompasses a large part of North Nashville—had the nation's highest percentage of incarcerated people born between 1980 and 1986.[3] These two seemingly disparate writings reflect the multifaceted current position of North Nashville—a position that simultaneously shows positive growth and persistent challenges.

The exhibition *Murals of North Nashville Now* and this accompanying publication seek to shine a light on this culturally rich yet often underserved and arguably overpoliced community through the presentation of eight newly commissioned murals made by a talented and ambitious group of young artists who live, work, or received their education in North Nashville. As residents of and visitors to Nashville know, a vibrant street art scene has emerged throughout the city in recent years alongside its rapid expansion, and murals can now be seen on walls in the Nations, the Gulch, along Nolensville Pike, and in other areas. Those found in North Nashville stand out because they are made by artists with strong ties to the neighborhood and because much of the imagery reflects its unique character.

Important murals have been made in North Nashville since 1930, when Harlem Renaissance great Aaron Douglas came to Fisk to create a series for Cravath Library (fig. 1). More recently, in 2012, artist James Threalkill and Tennessee State University professor Michael McBride were commissioned to mark the contentious area under the I-40 overpass at Jefferson Street with an extended series of murals (fig. 2) and, in 2015, Tennessee State University graduate Woke3 organized a major event called Norf Wall Fest that touched multiple parts of the neighborhood. With the assistance of a Metro Nashville Arts Commission THRIVE microgrant, Woke3 brought a selection of artists together, including his former professor Sam Dunson (fig. 3) and mentors Michael "Ol Skool" Mucker (fig. 4) and Thaxton Waters (fig. 5), to paint murals in an area under Jubilee Bridge and along Buchanan and Jefferson Streets. The Norf Art Collective, comprising Woke3 and fellow artists doughjoe, Sensei, and keep3, developed out of the festival. Norf is committed to producing public art that addresses social issues as well as the distinctive historical aspects of North Nashville.

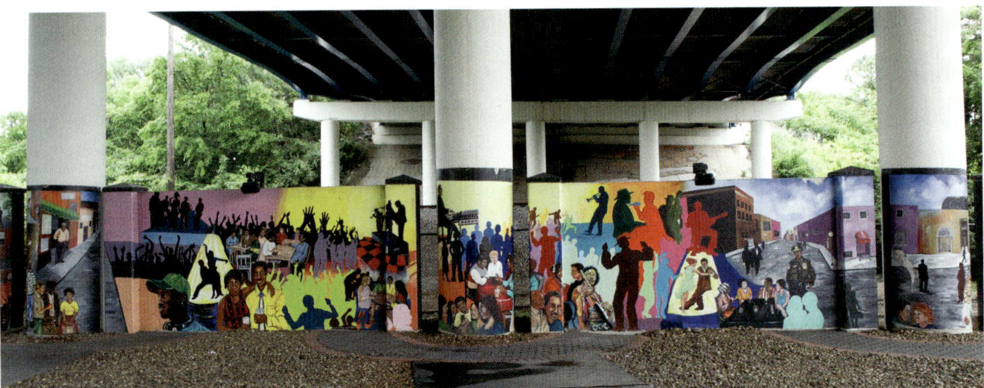

Figure 2
Michael McBride and James Threalkill. *Gateway to Heritage*, 2012. Located at Jefferson Street beneath the I-40 overpass. Created for the Gateway to Heritage Plaza. This project was a joint effort by the US Department of Housing and Urban Development, the Tennessee Department of Transportation, Tennessee State University, the Jefferson Street United Merchant Partnership, Metro Public Works, and the Metropolitan Housing and Development Agency. Supported by a Tennessee Department of Transportation Roadscapes grant with matching funds from Metro Nashville. Photo: keep3

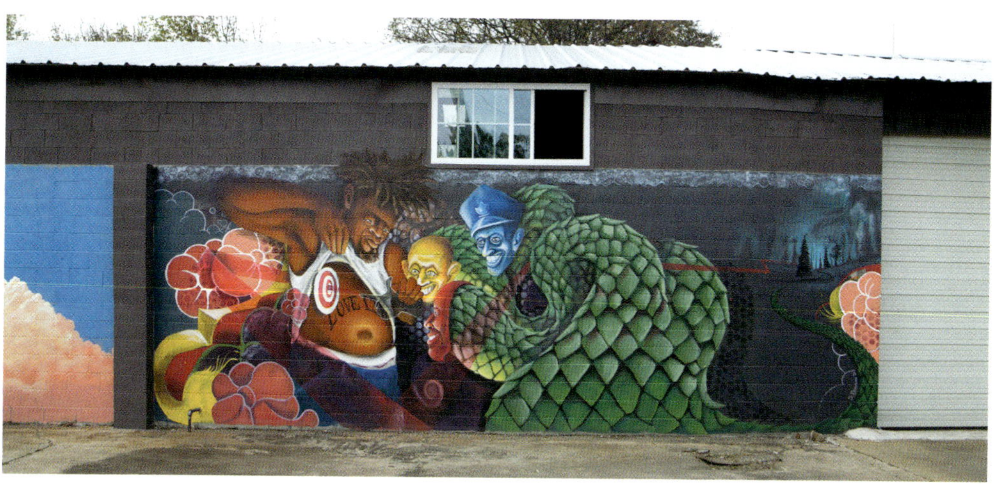

Figure 3
Sam Dunson. *Doubting Thomases*, 2015. Located at 808 19th Avenue North. Created for the Norf Wall Fest. This project was funded in part by the Metro Nashville Arts Commission THRIVE program. © Sam Dunson. Photo: keep3

For this exhibition, Norf Art Collective represents the children featured in their 2018 Clarksville Pike mural, *Family Matters* (page 29), as maturing individuals rising above negative situations and making plans for a healthy future, with education, community, and clean natural resources as necessary building blocks. Along with Norf, five individual artists were invited to make murals. Omari Booker highlights the gentrification caused by the current residential construction boom and the legacy of "redlining," discriminatory lending and investment policies promoted by banks and the Federal Housing Administration. Photographer and graphic designer LeXander Bryant offers alternatives to the narrow selection of career opportunities many African American children are exposed to as he attempts to transform minds with his own unabashed propaganda. Brandon Donahue commemorates local victims of violence by creating a memorial wall on which the name of each person killed in 2018 and early 2019 is airbrushed. Elisheba Israel Mrozik, who owns One Drop Ink and is an internationally known tattoo artist, focuses on the strength of women in particular as they navigate an environment filled with systemic inequities. XPayne, a graduate of Watkins College of Art, created a mural featuring a young superhero fighting off the dragon of greed under the direction of a stoic elder dressed as Batman.

McGruder Family Resource Center, housed in the former John Early School, has also contributed to the cultural landscape in recent years through artist residencies, workshops, and projects. Courtney Adair Johnson, Marlos E'van, and Nuveen Barwari worked with youth at the center through the International Teen Outreach Program at the Oasis Center and the mayor's paid internship program, Opportunity NOW, to create a collaborative mural, *Where we were. Where we are. Where we are going.*

Murals of North Nashville Now is the first exhibition devoted solely to local African American artists (aside from some participants in the community-made mural) at the Frist Art Museum. It offers insights into this valuable part of our city from the perspective of multiple young figures, all of whom are using their public work to address timely social issues, expand viewers' understanding of the past and present moment, and, ultimately, lift up their community.

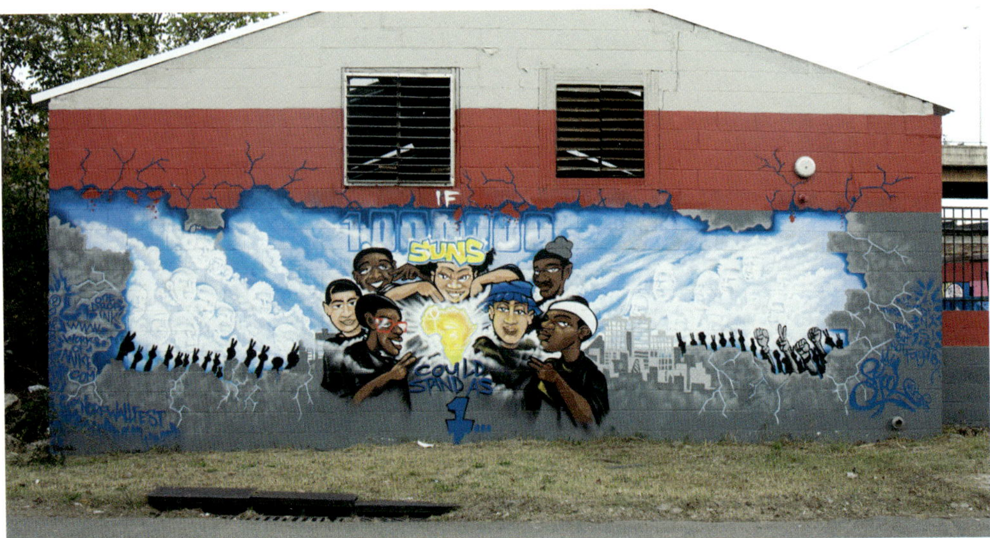

Figure 4
Ol Skool. *If One Million Suns Could Stand as One*, 2015. Located at 808 19th Avenue North. Created for the Norf Wall Fest. This project was funded in part by the Metro Nashville Arts Commission THRIVE program. © Ol Skool. Photo: keep3

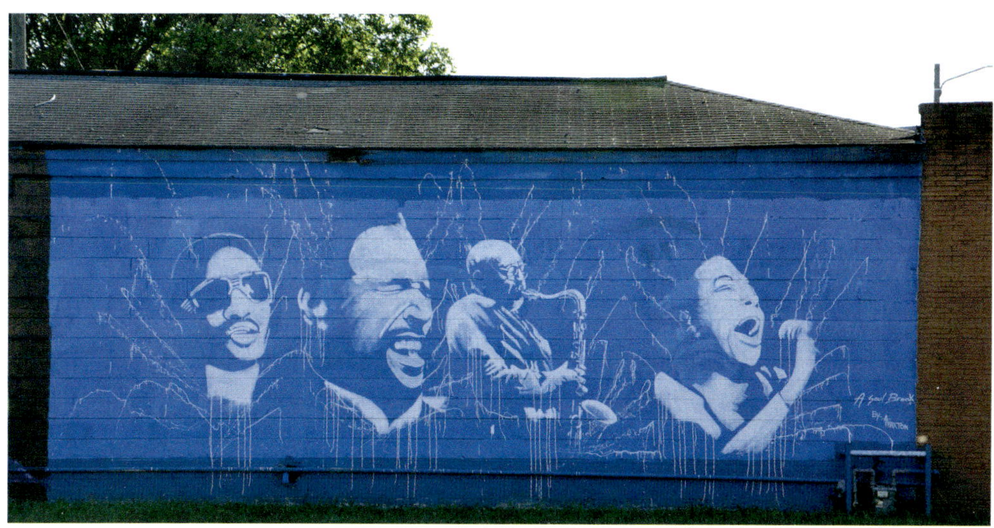

Figure 5
Thaxton Waters. *A Soul Break*, 2016. Located at 2615 Jefferson Street. © Thaxton Waters. Photo: Wallace Joiner

The exhibition and book also explore what role the arts can play in urban redevelopment and in the expression of neighborhood and individual identities, further testifying that art can be found all around us, not just inside museums and galleries.

Kathryn E. Delmez

NOTES

1. Erica Ciccarone, "Historically Black North Nashville Is Creating Cultural Spaces That Matter," *Nashville Scene*, April 26, 2018.

2. Steven Hale, "History Repeats Itself in North Nashville," *Nashville Scene*, June 7, 2018. Hale wrote a follow-up article for the *Nashville Scene*, "Making Peace" (June 25, 2019), that highlights the work of Gideon's Army, a grassroots activist organization devoted to preventing (or "interrupting," as they say) violence and mentoring North Nashville youth.

3. Adam Looney and Nichola Turner, "Work and Opportunity Before and After Incarceration," The Brookings Institution, March 2018. https://www.brookings.edu/wp-content/uploads/2018/03/es_20180314_looneyincarceration_final.pdf

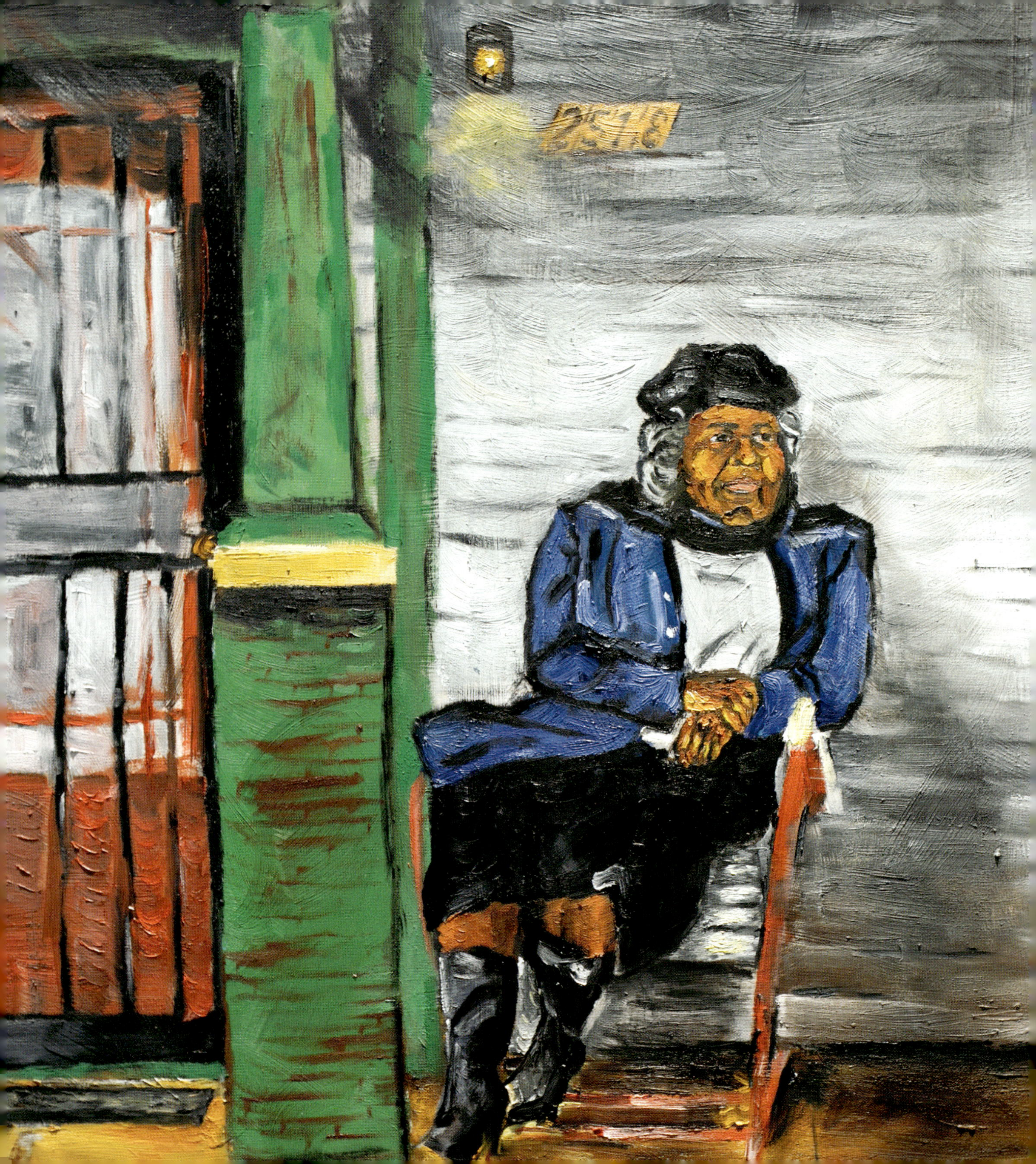

A BALM IN GILEAD: LOVE, HOPE, AND DESPAIR IN NORTH NASHVILLE

It's early Saturday morning at a home on Twelfth Avenue North in Nashville. A father wakes his young son and instructs him to get dressed. Although the sun has barely peeked over the tree line of the eastern bank of the Cumberland River, it is time to work. Things have been rough for his family of late. The nation is experiencing the most severe economic depression in its history, and it has finally hit home for him and many North Nashville families. In the past, he had steady work as a mechanic at the Nashville and Chattanooga Railroad's Roundhouse, but he is now unemployed. In an act of faith, he has purchased a truck and started a coal and ice company with plans to service North Nashville.

On this Saturday morning, they have several businesses awaiting the hundred-pound blocks of ice they will load onto the truck for two events, and many of the neighborhood churches have made similar requests for their Saturday programs and Sunday services. It is the 1930s, and this father is intent upon wringing a living for his family out of Depression-era Nashville despite having to compete with larger white-owned companies such as Fred B. Cassety's Coal and Coke Company and others in the city. For him and his family, life in North Nashville during the Great Depression is characterized by hope in the midst of a furious struggle for survival. Indeed, this had been true for African Americans and others who have lived in this area since its settlement in the late eighteenth century.

For much of Nashville's history the geographical area defined as North Nashville has fluctuated. Using the boundaries of the community established by early historians and local tradition, North Nashville extends from the Cumberland River in the east to Twenty-Eighth Avenue North in the west. Buchanan Street for many sits as its northernmost boundary while Charlotte Avenue (formerly Cedar Street) marks the southernmost border. The African American presence in this area—both as enslaved and free individuals—is as old as the history of the state. As James Robertson, John Donelson, and other settlers sought to wrest control of the land away from the indigenous populations who had called the area home, free and enslaved African Americans—a group whose descendants would one day represent more than 90 percent of North Nashville's population—participated actively in the contest, often fighting alongside and against their enslavers and the area's indigenous groups for ownership.[1]

Perhaps the first person to construct a permanent settlement in North Nashville was David McGavock, the son of a wealthy Virginian who arrived in the area and purchased more than 2,400 acres of land in 1786. Although McGavock purchased land on both sides of the Cumberland River, a significant portion on the eastern track (where he earned a profit from growing corn and cotton) occupied much of what is considered North Nashville today.[2] Germans began to migrate to the area in the 1830s, occupying the area just north of Jefferson Street between Fifth Avenue North and the river. Early arrivals of note include the prominent grocers John H. and Mary Ratterman Buddeke and Prussian-born architect Adolphus Heiman.[3]

For much of the nineteenth century, North Nashville would be a place of stark contrast; it was a space that symbolized Nashville's transition from a frontier town to a major Southern capital. Indeed, the areas that currently encompass North Nashville became a gateway to both enslavement and emancipation for many who found temporary lodging there. It became a place where freedom could begin for fugitives seeking to stow away on a steamer heading down the Cumberland toward the Ohio River, and a site of the involuntary breaking up of families for those whose arrival in the city would be followed by the dehumanizing experience of standing on an auction block.[4] No space in the city represented this more definitively than the almost quarter-mile stretch from Nashville's Public Square to Fourth Avenue North.

According to one early historian, Davidson County's "first court-house was built in 1803."[5] He also noted that county leaders located another institution and the objects needed to maintain the enslavement of African Americans there at the same time. The author notes, "The first jail was a one-story log house on the square, about twenty by thirty feet in size, and a whipping-post and pillory near by it."[6] From 1803 to 1861, the Public Square and the first five blocks of

Cedar Street (Charlotte Avenue) became one of the most important spaces in the city, as many of the businesses that grew up around them played integral roles in the introduction to and maintenance and control of enslaved African Americans. These businesses included the Planters and Union banks, institutions that provided generous terms on loans to purchase Tennessee's most valuable assets: land and enslaved blacks. It also included the Market House, a business where one could buy someone as young as seven years old on a credit of ten months, as long as the purchaser made payment with a note from the Union Bank. Indeed, potential profits, accompanied by physical pain and psychological trauma as a result of enslavement and emancipation, characterized North Nashville for much of the nineteenth century. Tennessee's withdrawal from the Union in 1861 and the disintegration of slavery in the Volunteer State radically changed the character of the community for the remainder of the century. It became one of the sites in the city where its citizens struggled to define liberty.

A new North Nashville emerged as Nashville entered into the twentieth century, although its relationship with the rest of the city would remain as schizophrenic as it had been in the past. It was a community that had experienced brief joy with the destruction of slavery, survived the terrorism of the Ku Klux Klan, and collectively steeled itself to confront the reality of Jim Crow segregation. Members of the community created and organized the secular and religious institutions that would be necessary for their survival and well-being in the twentieth century and beyond—institutions that influenced not only Nashville, but the entire world.

Among the most influential of these were its schools, churches, and businesses. Although often led by elite members of the North Nashville community, these institutions intersected in ways that both insulated its residents from some of the most harmful physical and psychological impacts of Jim Crow, and at the same time created an environment that undermined it. Further, they created an environment that established North Nashville as the stage where the struggle for black equality took shape. They also provided a home for many of

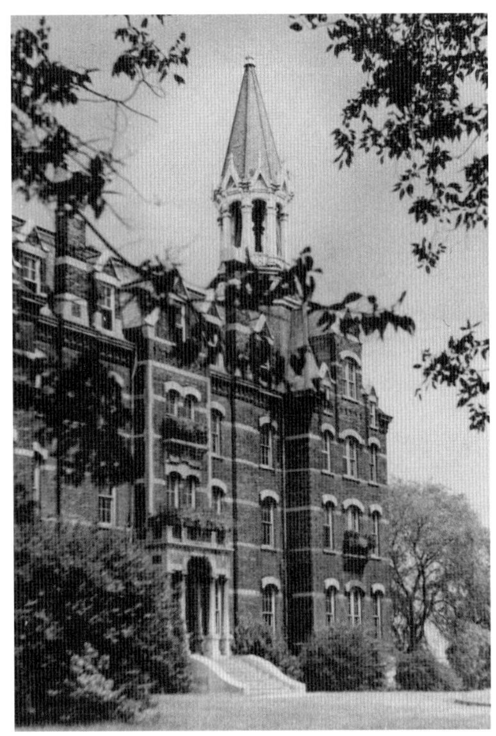

Figure 1
Jubilee Hall at Fisk University, n.d. Photograph. Fisk University Photograph Collection, ful.bul.pho080. Courtesy of Fisk University, John Hope and Aurelia E. Franklin Library, Special Collections, Julius Rosenwald Database, http://rosenwald.fisk.edu

the men and women whose lives would shape Nashville's identity into the twentieth century and beyond. Indeed, Nashville would not be Music City USA or the Athens of the South without North Nashville.

The three institutions in North Nashville that had the greatest effect on how residents negotiated and confronted Jim Crow were colleges and schools, the oldest being Fisk University. Fisk University opened on January 9, 1866, with the assistance of the American Missionary Association, the Western Freedman's Aid Commission, and the Bureau of Refugees, Freedmen, and Abandoned Lands.[7] The university would arrive at its current North Nashville location as a result of the efforts of the Fisk Jubilee Singers. The young students, led by young Fiskites such as Ella Sheppard, who was born into slavery, raised their voices—singing the spirituals their ancestors raised out of Tennessee's cotton and tobacco fields during enslavement—to earn money that would eventually lead to the dedication of Jubilee Hall in 1876. Jubilee Hall became the first permanent building in the United States created for the education of African Americans, and it remains one of the most arresting architectural structures in Music City (fig.1).[8]

Tennessee State University opened its doors to students on June 19, 1912. Welcoming students to its campus as the Tennessee A&I State Normal School for Negroes, the new school—along with nearby Hadley Park, the first park in America created exclusively for African Americans—stood in the minds of many whites as shining examples of the efficacy of Jim Crow segregation. However, the notion that the newly created school could be used by Tennessee as a symbol that highlighted the state's compliance with Supreme Court Case *Plessy v. Ferguson* proved to be an illusion. As one of only two land-grant colleges in the Volunteer State, Tennessee State University never received equitable funding. Hattie Ewing Hale, faculty member and wife of Tennessee A&I's first president, William Jasper Hale, recalled, "The school was created where the adverse sentiment for its mere presence made for an attitude of intense struggle just to survive."[9]

Meharry Medical College arrived in North Nashville in 1931. Created in 1876 as the medical division of Central Tennessee College, Meharry's move to North Nashville placed it within a stone's throw of Fisk University, which for much of the school's history had been its northern rival in Music City. Meharry Medical College quickly became one of the most important institutions in North Nashville because the school and its associated hospital trained doctors and provided access to healthcare for Nashville's entire African American community. Meharry's service to the community continues today, as it remains one of the leading producers of African American scientists, physicians, and dentists in the world.[10]

The presence of Fisk and Tennessee A&I contributed not only to the economic growth of the area prior to the 1920s—building upon a core group of elite black Nashvillians who had a presence there dating back to the nineteenth century it also fostered a greater awareness of the goings-on at the two schools among many in the community. While news of a pending class of graduates from Tennessee A&I made its way down the thoroughfare and caused excitement at the prospect of new teachers in their community, other reports were the cause of concern. News in 1924 of the lights in Livingstone Hall on Fisk's campus burning long past curfew, tales of heavy-handed Nashville policemen, and students facing possible expulsion over their displeasure with the strict governance by the university's white president, Fayette McKenzie, increased concern about the students' well-being among members of the community.[11] Many of the street's residents had recent memories of police brutality and arbitrary arrests, and ultimately came to support the plight of the Fisk students in their battle with the university's president. David Levering Lewis notes in his biography of W. E. B. DuBois, who returned to his alma mater to speak in support of the students, that the community opened its doors to the Fisk students who were no longer welcomed in its dormitory or dining halls because of the protest.[12]

This concern with the well-being of the students would continue into the future, and African Americans in North Nashville would rally to assist them when they were in need, with many opening up their homes to students from Fisk, Tennessee State, and Meharry when the schools had insufficient student housing to accommodate them. Some families took in as many as three or four students, allowing them free access to their homes as well as use of the kitchen and other

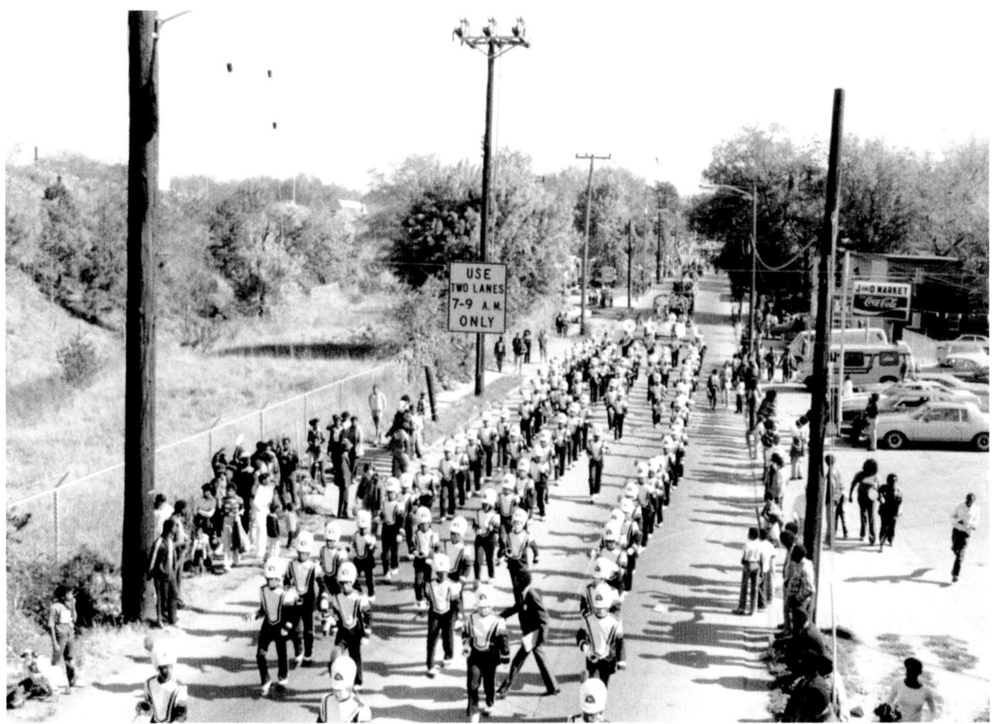

Figure 2
Tennessee State University Homecoming Parade, 1980. Photograph. Fisk University, Jefferson Street Photograph Project Collection. Courtesy of Fisk University, John Hope and Aurelia E. Franklin Library, Special Collections, Julius Rosenwald Database, http://rosenwald.fisk.edu

areas. These actions cultivated an intimate relationship between the students and the community; according to one longtime resident, many of the students preferred boarding with the families in the community over life in the dorms.[13]

Tennessee A&I also strengthened its ties with the North Nashville community when it began scheduling its annual homecoming games on Thanksgiving Day (fig. 2). Having homecoming and the football game on Thanksgiving Day made the events family affairs that included alumni, students, and North Nashville families alike. More importantly, they provided a surge in revenue for the businesses in the community. The annual parade would meander through North Nashville, but the route would always incorporate a significant stretch of Jefferson Street before ending on campus, thus giving the businesses an opportunity to display their wares along the parade route. Later that afternoon, family members young and old would make their way to campus to watch their Tigers pummel their opponents into submission.

The importance of the Thanksgiving Day homecoming celebration and other activities at Fisk, A&I, and Meharry should not be underestimated. Big events on campus brought much-needed cash into North Nashville's economy. The dressmakers, barbers, beauticians, nightclubs, and liquor store owners could boast of an increase in sales that might arguably rival revenue received during the Christmas and Easter seasons. Similarly, hotel and restaurant owners would have likely enjoyed comparable increases in revenue.

Scholars of Nashville history and former residents have long cited Jefferson Street, the major thoroughfare through the community, as the space that demonstrated the economic potential of North Nashville. Jefferson Street's music scene was legendary, and one could go to its many clubs and venues to catch performances by acclaimed blues, rhythm and blues, and jazz greats.[14] Its churches and schools played an important role in its transition from a low-income to a middle- and working-class neighborhood, but arguably its greatest economic growth coincided with the beginning of the Great Depression. Historian Bobby Lovett points out in his study of Nashville's African American elites that after the stock market

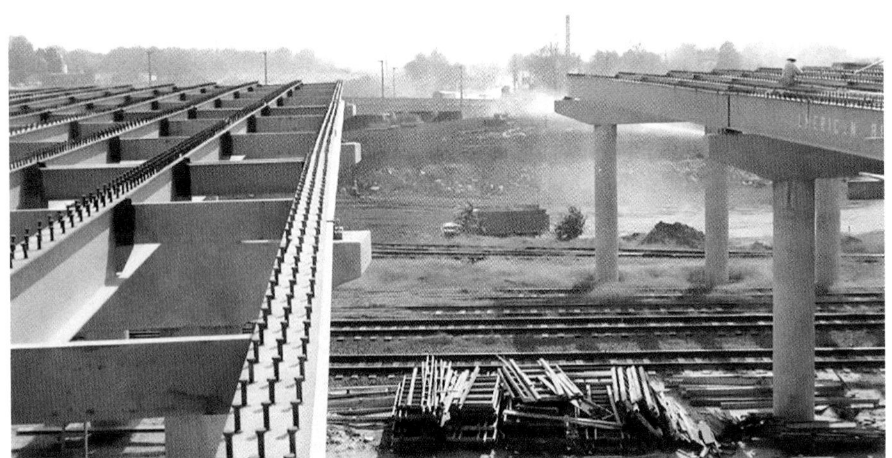

Figure 3
Construction of Interstate 40, ca. 1968. Photograph. Courtesy of Metro Historical Commission

crash, middle-class African Americans began to find Jefferson Street more attractive and that their businesses tended to do better there in the shadows of the city's three historically black colleges and universities as the Great Depression dragged along.

Close scrutiny of the residents living on Jefferson Street does not, however, provide a clear picture of why these businesses continued to operate well into the 1960s. According to the 1960 Federal Census, North Nashville blacks still held the same menial jobs that they had before, but in this instance their economic outlook seemed much worse than their forebears because of the persistence of the economic downturn. Yet, two things worthy of note quickly emerge, especially when one considers plans made by the state for an interstate route during the post-WWII years, a stretch that would carry the highway through sections of the most economically well-off parts of the community (fig. 3). On the Jefferson Street blocks with the greatest number of households—the 1200 and 2600 blocks, respectively—homeowners outnumbered renters by a ratio of almost two to one.[15] But on these two blocks, the homes—many of which were constructed during the Great Depression—and their residents would cease to be a part of the community in less than a generation because of Interstate 40. Their departure would have a catastrophic effect on a community that was already struggling. For example, in areas only a stone's throw from the campuses of Fisk and Meharry, in 1950, between 50 and 70 percent of the households lived below the poverty line. In 2017, poverty in the area exceeded 60 percent.[16]

Still, in the midst of the despair that accompanied most of North Nashville's poverty-stricken areas, Jefferson Street stood as a shining thread of hope. The intersection of Twenty-Eighth Avenue North and Jefferson Street served as a gateway to a thriving African American business district, with many businesspersons being sensitive to the plight of the community. For example, residents who had little money and could not afford coal during Nashville's chilly nights during the Depression could count on the willingness of the "Coal and Ice Man" to barter so that they could heat their homes and refrigerate food.[17] African American performers whose tours brought them to Music City inevitably made their way to Jefferson Street, to sing, play, or relax and escape the dehumanizing effects of Jim Crow in one of the street's many boarding houses and hotels. At the corner of Eighteenth and Jefferson Street, Flem Otey, a former Pullman car cook, transformed the busy intersection into the Otey Center. The center housed Otey's grocery, the first African American grocery in Nashville, a laundromat, and a realty company. As was the case with the Otey Center, many of Jefferson Street's most successful businesses tended to be located where the street intersected major avenues. The corner of Twenty-Eighth and Jefferson had a pharmacy, cleaners, filling station, and shoe repair.

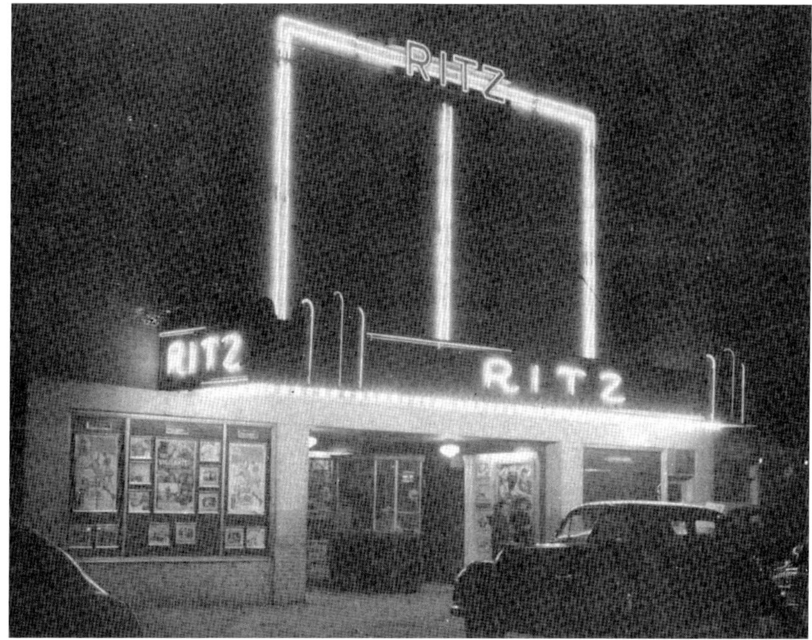

Figure 4
Frank O. Roberts. Ritz Theater, 1951. Photograph. Published in the 1951 Fisk Oval Yearbook. Courtesy of Fisk University, John Hope and Aurelia E. Franklin Library, Special Collections, Julius Rosenwald Database, http://rosenwald.fisk.edu

During the 1940s, Jefferson Street could boast of having the city's only black fire company, a movie theater where African Americans could enjoy a movie without being Jim Crowed (fig. 4), and places where patrons could drink and gamble, such as the Club Del Morocco. In 1954, James Crowley moved his successful ten-chair barbershop from Fourth Avenue North to Jefferson Street where he occupied a magnificent building constructed by the African American architectural firm McKissack and McKissack. Kossie Gardner became the first of several funeral directors to move to the street, and he and Jefferson Street's other morticians worked to make sure that bereaved African American family members could take one last dignified ride through the streets of North Nashville.

For many years North Nashville provided a space where African American women—remarkable women like Georgia Boyd, who worked in the shadows of their famous North Nashville husbands—could hone their skills as organizers and activists.[18] These women played prominent roles in the schools, churches, homes, and businesses that passed down the cultural skills necessary for the community to negotiate the boundaries established by Jim Crow. Indeed, North Nashville in many ways served as a sanctuary from Jim Crow for many that lived, worked, studied, and played in the community. Conversely, it would also play a role in the dismantling of segregation when residents rallied behind students from Tennessee State, Fisk, American Baptist College (another HBCU approximately four miles northeast of Fisk), and Meharry when they organized to confront generations of discriminatory practices in Nashville businesses. As the community shuddered in the aftermath of the 1960 bombing that almost destroyed the home of attorney Z. Alexander Looby and his wife, Grafta, students marched down its streets to challenge Mayor Ben West to reconcile his views on race. During the 1960s, the eyes of the world focused on the activism emerging out of North Nashville.

Ironically, it was during the years following the Nashville Movement and its apparent success that North Nashville would face its greatest challenge. Many of the questions Diane Nash asked of Ben West on that fateful day in April 1960 appeared to have been answered, but as Nashville enters into the third decade of the twenty-first century, several of the problems that concerned its residents persist.[19] Despite the trauma inflicted upon the community by the interstate and the departure of many of its working- and middle-class families, businesses on and around Jefferson Street have rallied in an attempt to revive the community. The Jefferson Street United Merchants Partnership (JUMP) has initiated a sustained effort to revitalize the community and Jefferson Street's business corridor. Today the more than 111 individuals and businesses that make up the organization celebrate Jefferson Street's rich history as a music district and work as advocates for diversified investment in the community. JUMP sponsors annual jazz and blues and African heritage festivals that draw tens of thousands to Nashville in a celebration of the music and vibrant activity that made the neighborhood famous. Housing remains an issue for many in the community, and many long-term residents are falling victim to the rising tide of gentrification that has accompanied Nashville's recent growth. Similarly, poverty remains a common feature of the areas near Fisk and Meharry. The poor in North Nashville inhabit a world that seems to be created and defined by outsiders. While many in the city look back and celebrate its historic thriving businesses and the contribution its culture has made to the Music City's identity, North Nashville remains a world whose inhabitants' lives and culture are often marginalized, ignored, and misrepresented by the larger society.

This exhibition and book present visitors and residents of Music City an opportunity to take an intimate view of North Nashville through the eyes of some of its most gifted residents. These artists, some of whom I am honored to number among my friends, have dazzled me with their creativity and work since my arrival in Nashville almost a decade ago. Their work is reflective of the community's history. Some murals will make viewers smile about the community's past and perhaps shed a tear over what has been lost over the past half century. In some instances they may inspire joy, and in others cause disgust, anger, or despair about the community's fate. In short, the artists' work allows viewers an opportunity to experience the community in a way that is unprecedented in Nashville history.

Learotha Williams Jr.

NOTES

1. Cynthia Cumfer, *Separate Peoples, One Land: The Minds of Cherokees, Blacks, and Whites on the Tennessee Frontier* (Chapel Hill: The University of North Carolina Press, 2007).

2. W. W. Clayton, *History of Davidson County, Tennessee, with Illustrations and Biographical Sketches of Its Prominent Men and Pioneers* (Philadelphia: J. W. Lewis, 1880), 425.

3. John Lawrence Connelly, "Old North Nashville and Germantown," *Tennessee Historical Quarterly* 39, no. 2 (Summer 1980): 119–23.

4. Bobby Lovett, *The African American History of Nashville, Tennessee, 1780–1930: Elites and Dilemmas* (Fayetteville: University of Arkansas Press, 1999).

5. Clayton, *History of Davidson County*, 196.

6. Ibid.

7. Joe M. Richardson, *A History of Fisk University 1865–1946* (Tuscaloosa: University of Alabama Press, 1980), 28–29.

8. Richardson, *History of Fisk University*, 39; *Fisk University: History, Building and Site, and Services of Dedication, at Nashville Tennessee, January 1st, 1876* (New York: Trustees of Fisk University, 1876), 7–8.

9. Bobby Lovett, *A Touch of Greatness: A History of Tennessee State University* (Macon, Georgia: Mercer University Press, 2012), 43.

10. Charles V. Roman, *Meharry Medical College: A History* (Nashville: Sunday School Pub. Board of the National Baptist Convention, Inc., 1934), 26.

11. Fisk students protested the policies of its president, Fayette McKenzie, in 1924–25. For more information, see Richardson, *History of Fisk University*.

12. David Levering Lewis, *W. E. B. DuBois: The Fight for Equality and the American Century, 1919–1963* (New York: Holt Paperbacks, 2001), 141.

13. Interview with Gloria Johnson, September 23, 2010. North Nashville Heritage Project.

14. Performers on Jefferson Street included musical greats such as Jimi Hendrix, Aretha Franklin, Count Basie, Muddy Waters, Otis Redding, Ray Charles, B. B. King, James Brown, and Etta James. Local talents such as Marion Jones, Billy Cox, and others were frequent performers on Jefferson Street.

15. The value of the homes in 1930 averaged $3,800 on the 1200 block, compared to $1,500 on the 2600 block, which was closest to Tennessee A&I. Rent in both areas averaged about $15 a month.

16. 1950 Census, *Housing Census Report*, volume 5, part 118 (Washington, DC: US Government Printing Office, 1952). Carmen DeNavas-Walt, Bernadette D. Proctor, and Jessica C. Smith, *Income, Poverty, and Health Insurance Coverage in the United States: 2008* (Washington, DC: US Census Bureau, 2009); Carmen DeNavas-Walt, Bernadette D. Proctor, and Jessica C. Smith, *Income, Poverty, and Health Insurance Coverage in the United States: 2010* (Washington, DC: US Census Bureau, 2011); Carmen DeNavas-Walt, Bernadette D. Proctor, and Jessica C. Smith, *Income, Poverty, and Health Insurance Coverage in the United States: 2012* (Washington, DC: US Census Bureau, 2013). US Census Bureau, *Social Explorer Tables: ACS 2017* (5-Year Estimates), https://socialexplorer.com/tables/ACS2017_5yr/R12192773. Accessed June 12, 2019.

17. Interview with Jesse Fanroy, September 14, 2010. North Nashville Heritage Project.

18. Georgia Boyd was married to Nashville businessperson and *Nashville Globe* publisher and editor Henry Allen Boyd. The Boyd family also chartered the National Baptist Publishing Board in 1898, which published hymnals, Sunday School books, and other religious materials for Baptists around the globe. Under her husband's leadership, the company became the largest black publisher in the United States.

19. While standing in front of more than 3000 protestors who accompanied her to Nashville's Public Square that day, Diane Nash asked Mayor Ben West if he believed it was wrong to discriminate against a person solely because of their race or color. West replied that he did.

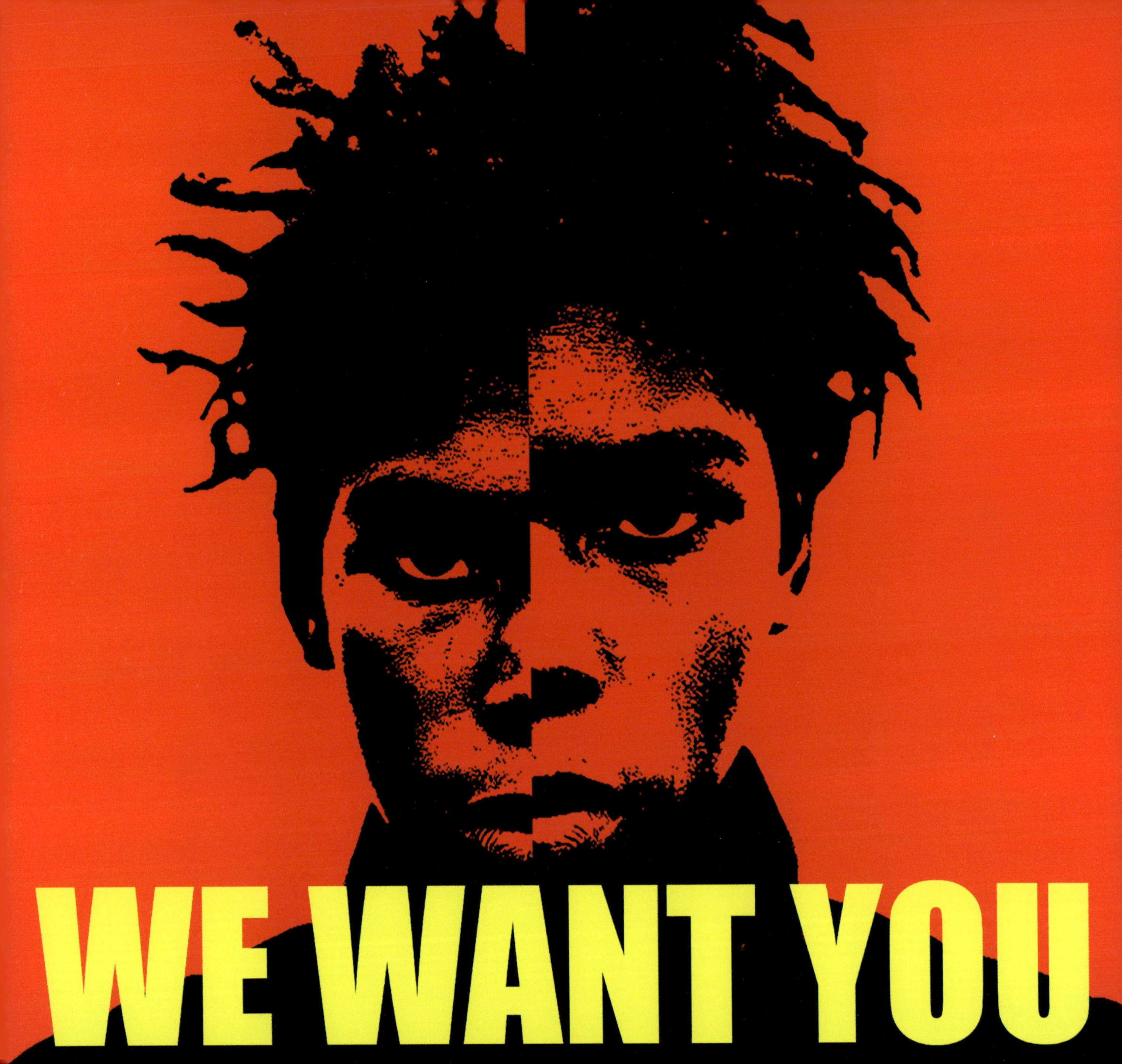
WE WANT YOU
WE'RE LOOKING FOR A TEAM OF SELF MOTIVATED INDIVIDUALS
WHO ARE COMMITTED TO BUILDING A SELF-SUFFICIENT COMMUNITY
THAT THRIVES ON LOVE, INNOVATION AND COMMERCE.
DO US A FAVOR AND HELP SPREAD THE WORD!

ARTIST ENTRIES

NORF ART COLLECTIVE

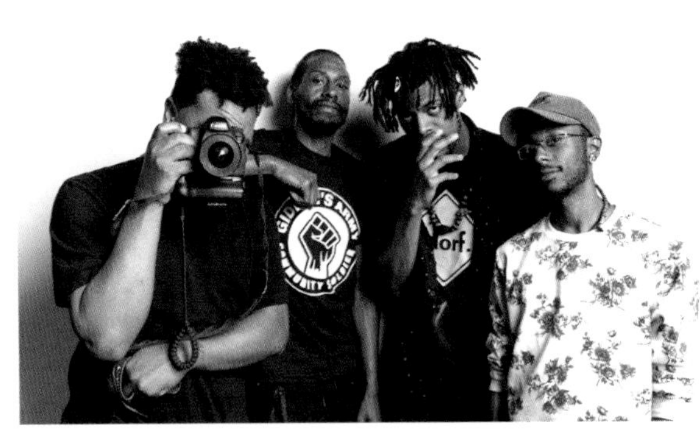

The Norf Art Collective is a team of multidisciplinary creatives, with artists Woke3, doughjoe, Sensei, and keep3 at its core. The collective was developed after a 2015 wall fest in North Nashville conceived by Woke3. As reflected in its name, Norf draws attention to and honors African American cultural specificities and history while also addressing current social issues. Although members are concerned about inequities of the past and about changes taking place in North Nashville now, a spirit of triumph pervades Norf projects.

Their large-scale mural *Family Matters* (page 29) on Clarksville Pike is a tribute to local 1960s civil rights figures Curlie McGruder, Diane Nash, John Lewis, and Z. Alexander Looby. Accompanying these figures are two children representing the next generation of activists. In a pair of newly created works for the exhibition, *Fly* (at right) and *Forever* (page 28), the children are maturing. In *Fly*, the boy's eyeglasses now fit his head, and his pacifier has fallen out; he sees clearly and no longer needs a crutch as he rises above negative situations such as the game of the streets and unbridled development. A streetlamp shines a light on these elements as well as on three young black men positioned within a passion flower, Tennessee's state wildflower. These men symbolize the many native North Nashvillians who are being pushed out by outsiders. Taken a step further, they can be read as a commentary on the intersectionality of African American lives with Native American experiences and the history of displacement in the region.

The girl in *Forever*, still wearing a yellow dress and flip-flops but no longer holding her teddy bear, is making plans for a healthy future, with education, community, creativity, and clean natural resources as necessary building blocks. She is writing the word *Norf* within the imagery as she strides toward a brighter world.

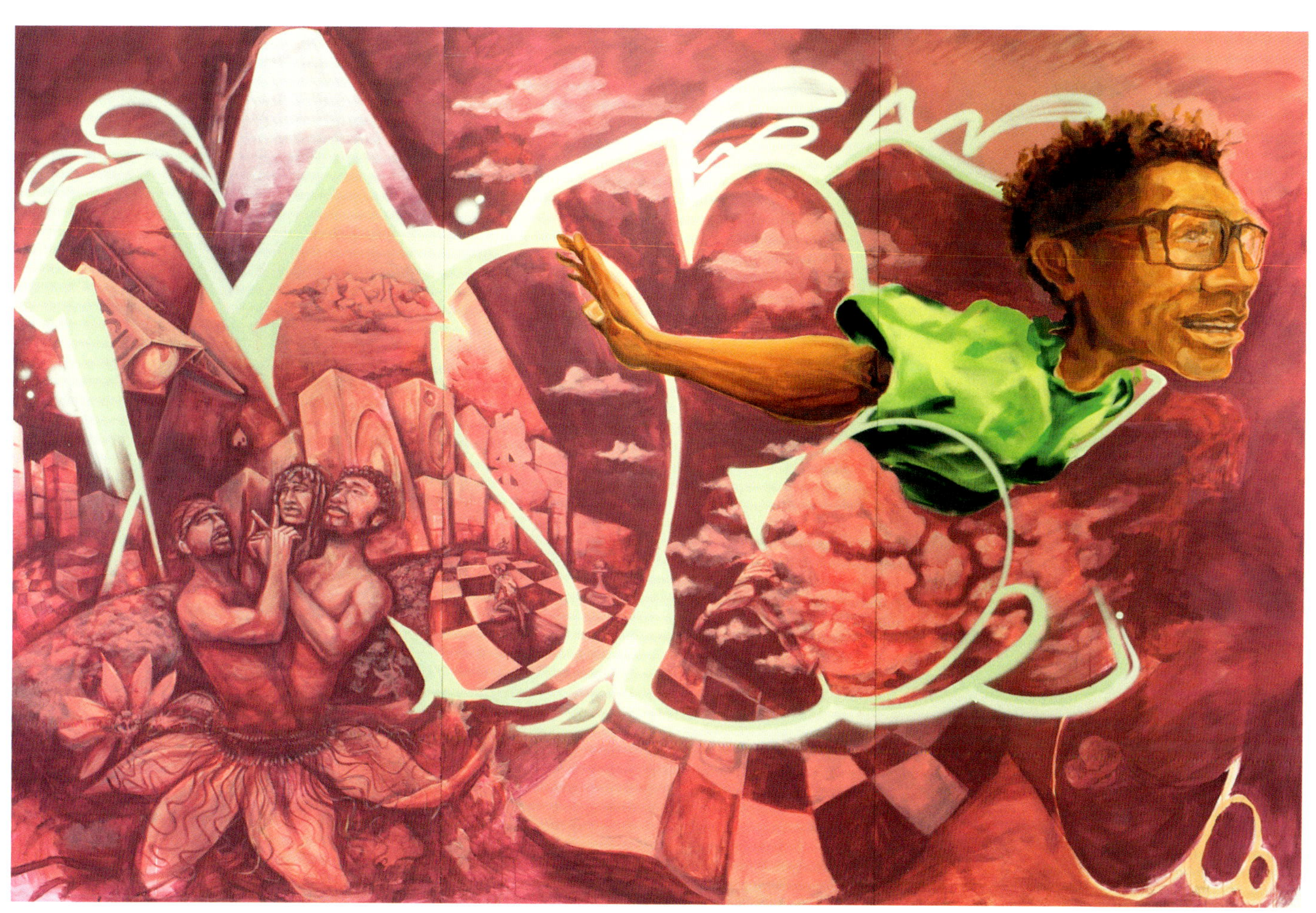

Fly, 2019
Acrylic spray paint, acrylic, and oil on panel

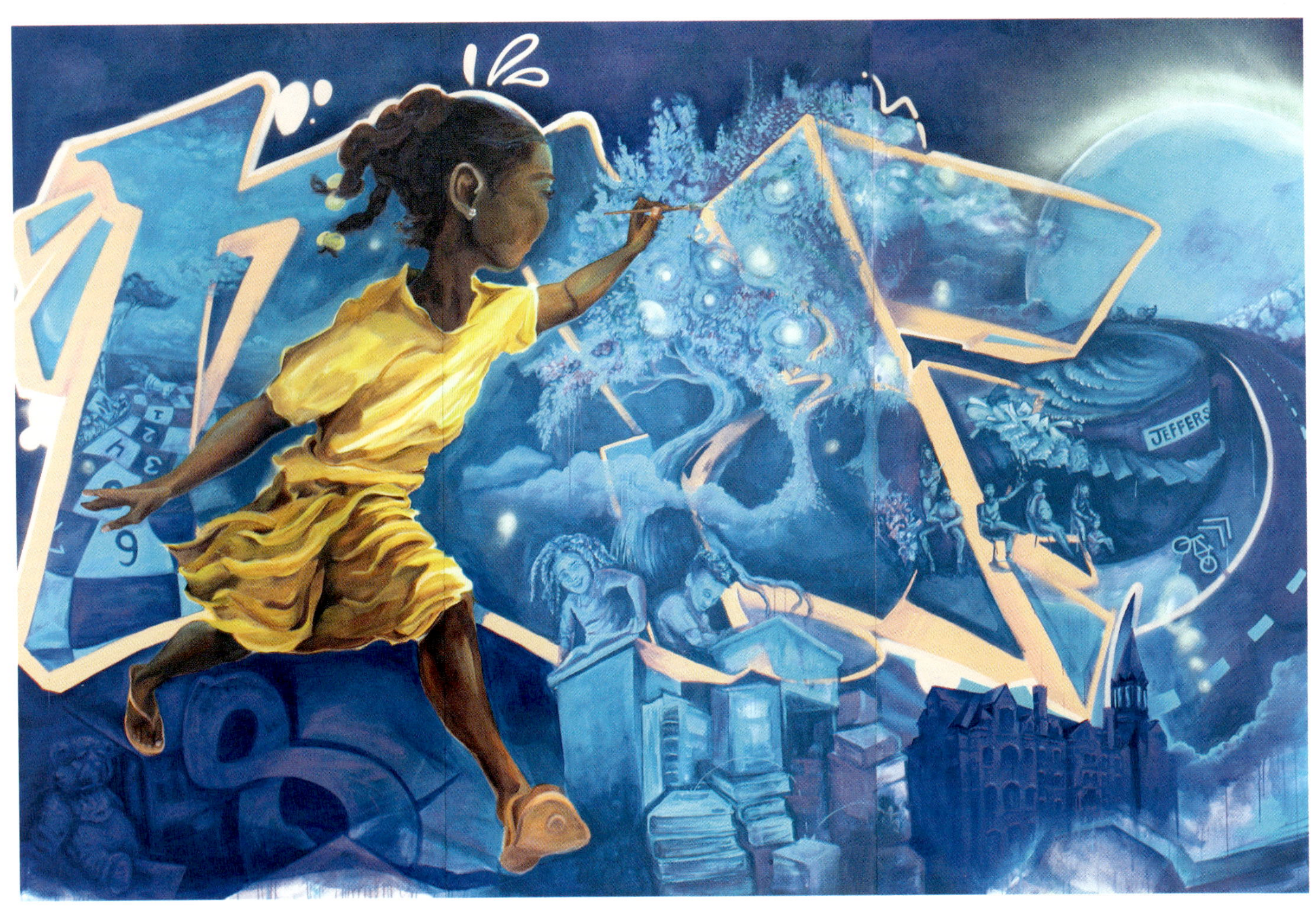

Forever, 2019
Acrylic spray paint, acrylic, and oil on panel

OTHER WORK

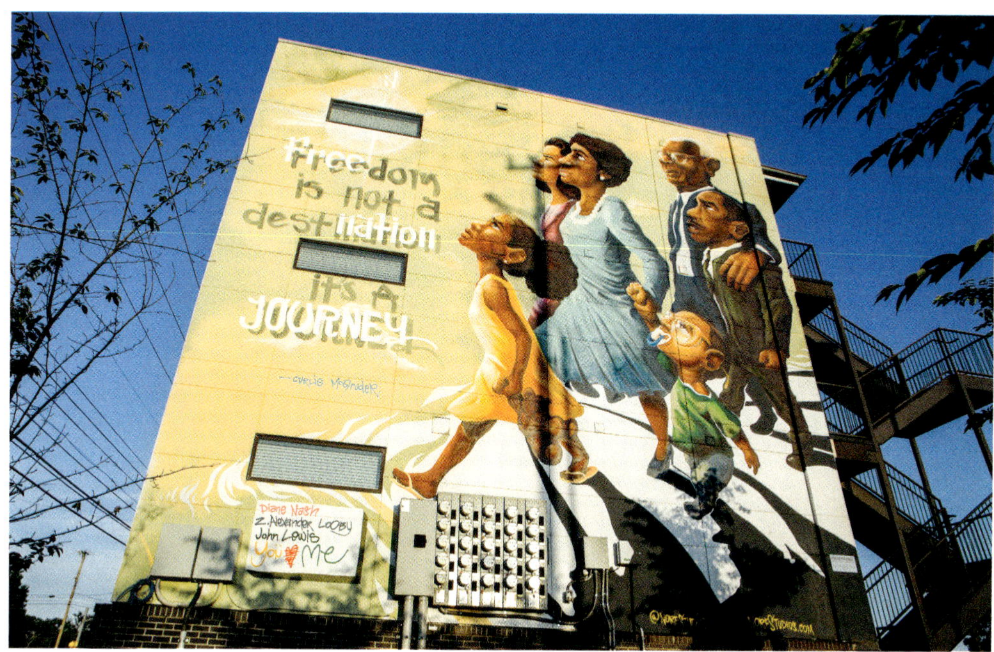

Norf Art Collective. *Family Matters*, 2017. Located at 2615 Clarksville Pike. Completed in partnership with Urban Housing Solutions and sponsored by Google Fiber. © Norf Art Collective. Photo: keep3

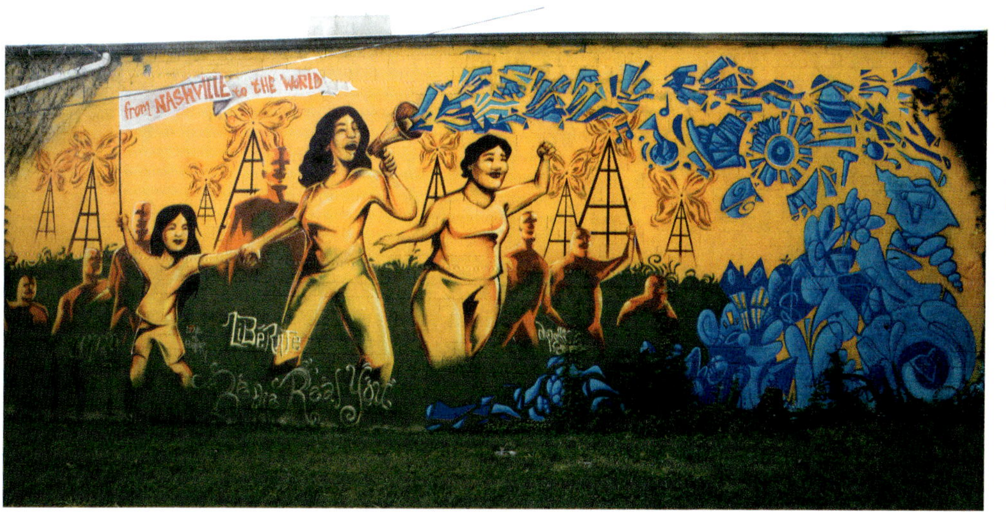

Norf Art Collective. *From Nashville to the World*, 2018. Located at 335 Whitsett Road. Completed in partnership with Workers' Dignity and radio 104.1 WDYO, and funded in part by the Metro Nashville Arts Commission THRIVE program. © Norf Art Collective. Photo: keep3

ELISHEBA ISRAEL MROZIK

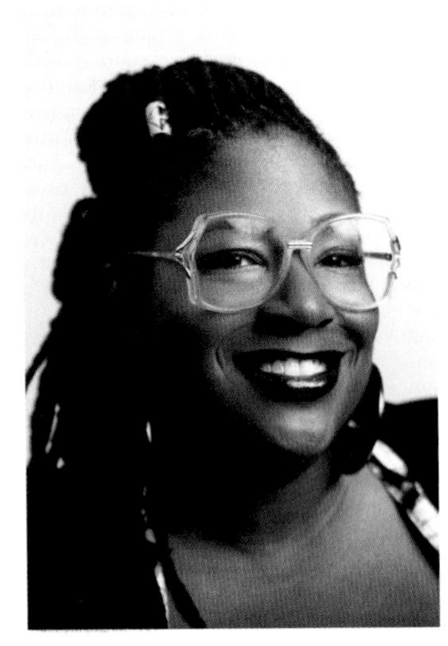

Memphis-native Elisheba Israel Mrozik focuses on revealing the strength of African American women as they navigate an environment filled with systemic inequities, incomplete histories, and racially motivated violence. The central figure of *Unmask 'Em* is a mother draped in royal purple, cradling the child she rears in one arm and the grown son, brother, or partner she buries in the other. The haloed trio becomes a contemporary Holy Family or Pietà scene. The blue-robed figure on the right, representing the establishment, is whitewashing an American history book by removing and burning depictions of African American heroes and lynchings. A dog, loyal to his master who wears a red robe made from the Tennessee state flag, peeks out of its blindfold while holding scales, suggesting bias and inequity in the judicial system. The figure in white watches but shrugs with a "not my problem" gesture while green-clad ghouls—symbols of greed and of the money propping up institutional injustice—stare blankly at visitors. Above the scene, the Nashville skyline has been placed in a bubble that is perhaps about to pop.

Mrozik's practice shifted from graphic design to tattooing eight years ago, when she opened One Drop Ink Tattoo Parlour on Jefferson Street. Now in an expanded space (still on Jefferson), the parlor also serves as a cultural hub in North Nashville; its gallery space, along with Woodcuts Gallery & Framing and the Garden Brunch Café, is an anchor of the monthly Jefferson Street Art Crawl.

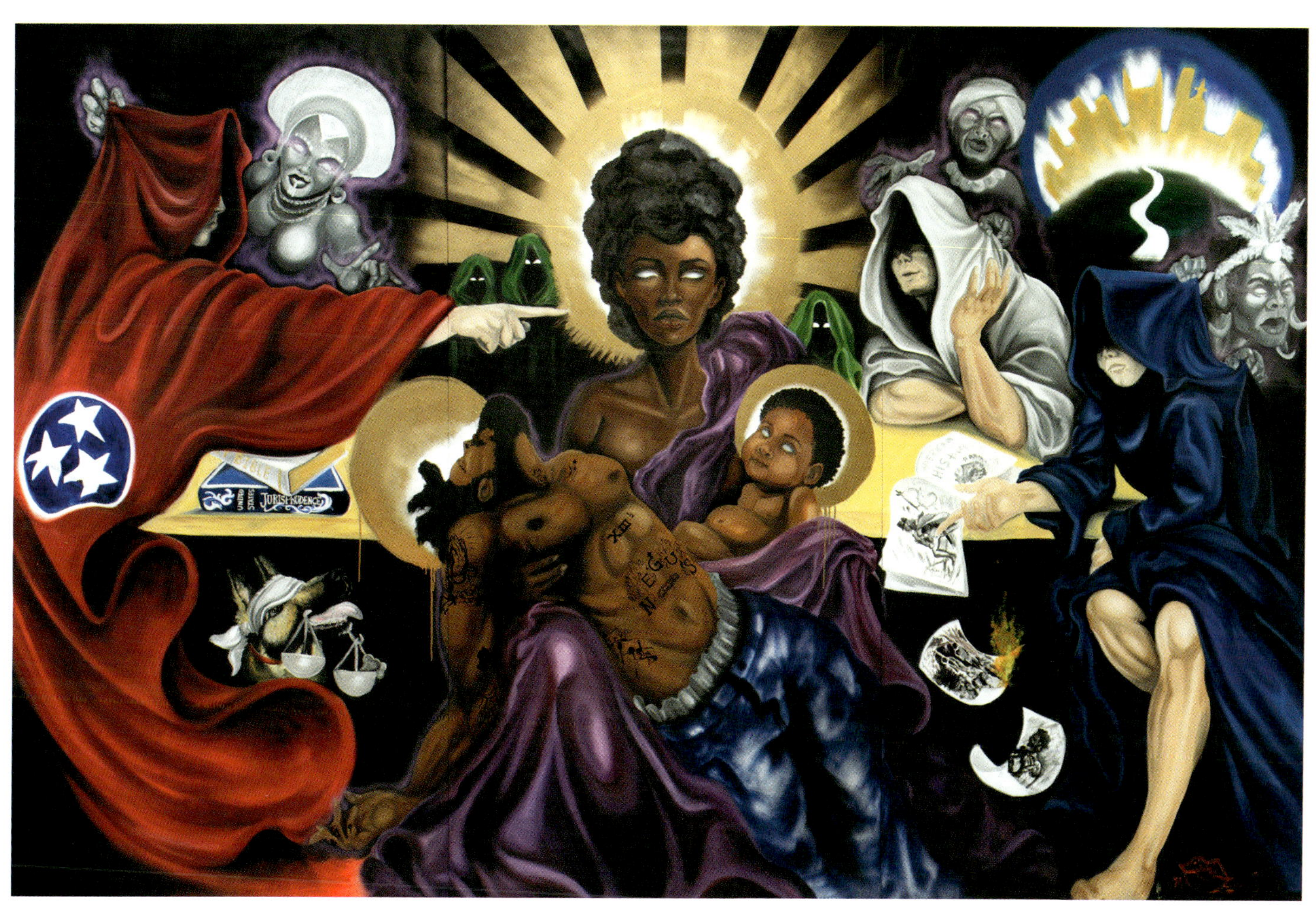

Unmask 'Em, 2019
Acrylic on panel

OTHER WORK

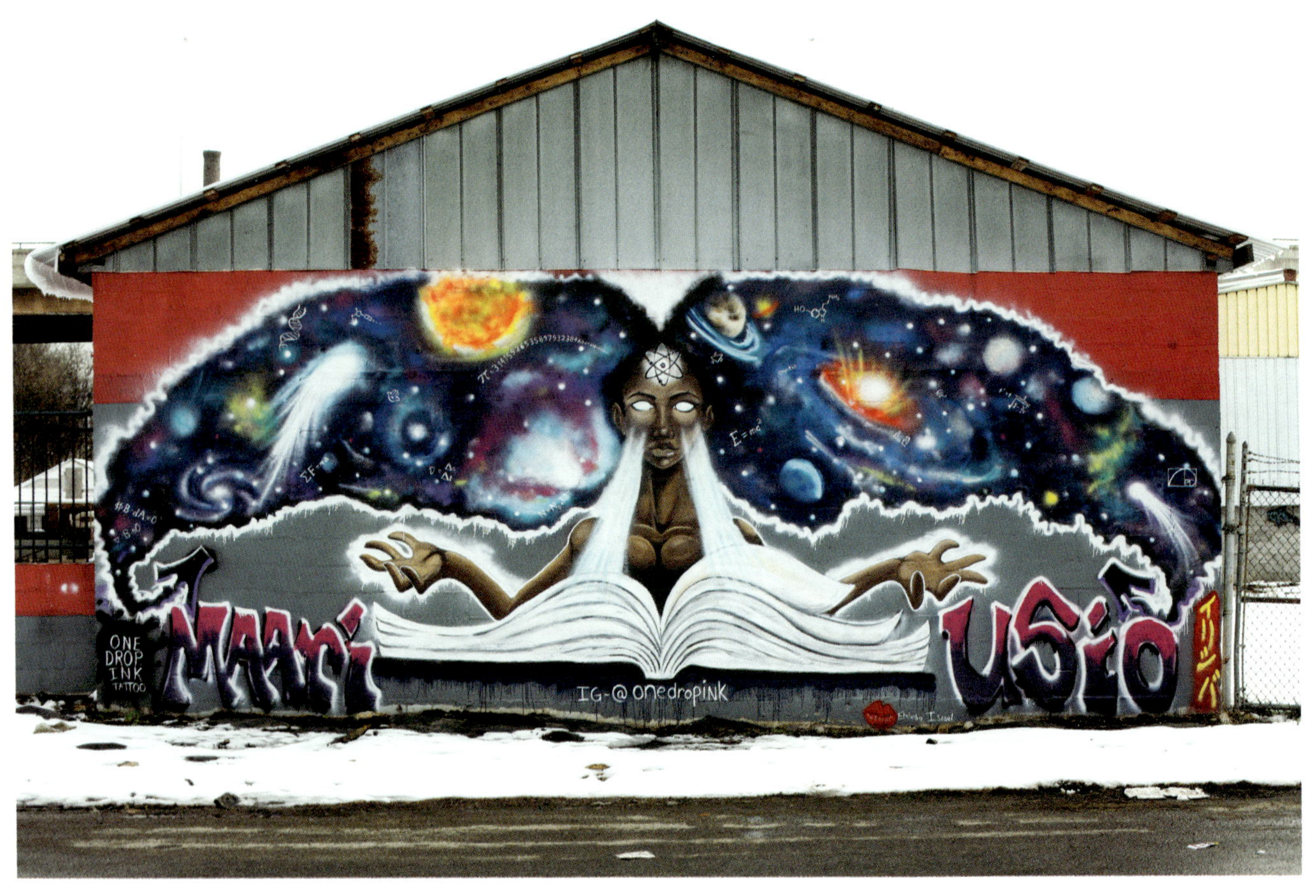

Elisheba Israel Mrozik. *Maari Usio*, 2015. Located at 808 19th Avenue North. Created for the Norf Wall Fest. This project was funded in part by the Metro Nashville Arts Commission THRIVE program. © Elisheba Israel Mrozik. Photo: John Russell

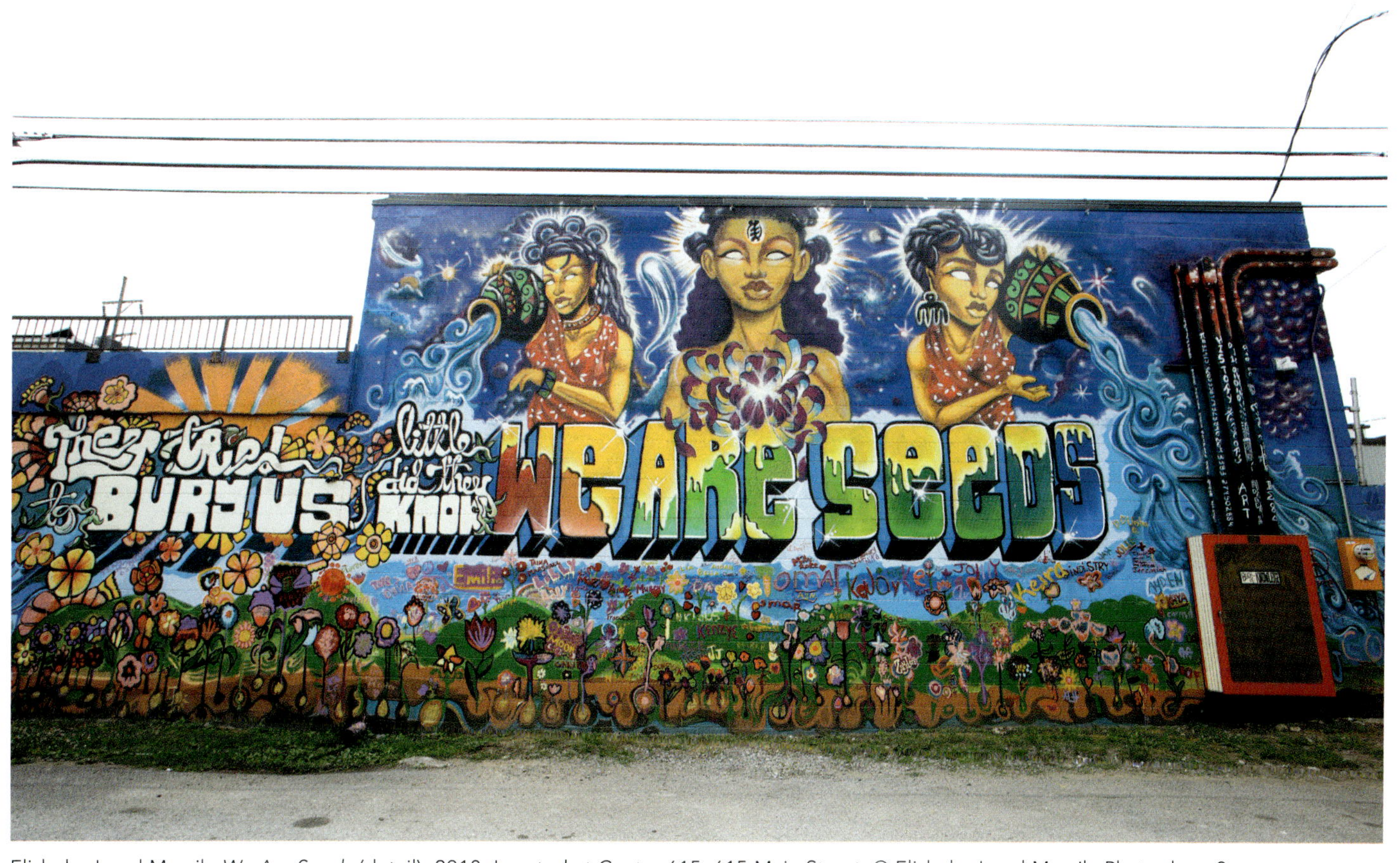

Elisheba Israel Mrozik. *We Are Seeds* (detail), 2018. Located at Center 615, 615 Main Street. © Elisheba Israel Mrozik. Photo: keep3

LEXANDER BRYANT

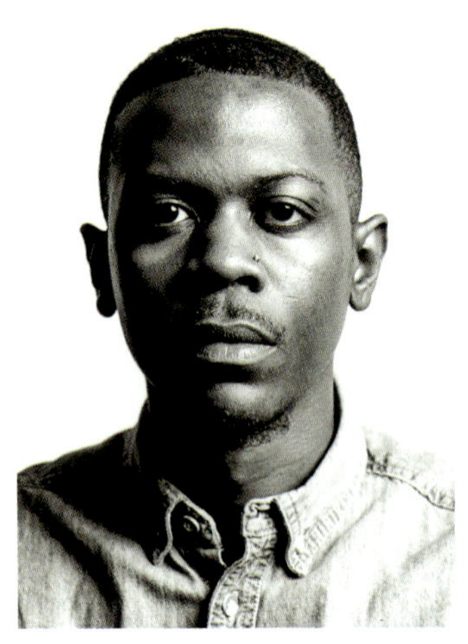

Photographer and graphic designer LeXander Bryant combines his own images and text to create overt propaganda meant to re-brainwash and transform the minds of viewers with messages like "Do Not Alter" and "Love Yourself Love Your Enemy," which elevate the value of black lives. The title *OPPORTUNITY CO$T* corresponds to an economic term used when assessing the financial implications of decision-making—in this case, the price a person pays when making a career choice without being aware of all options. The resulting loss of potential gain is beyond monetary. Under the penetrating eyes of an African American boy and the familiar armed services recruiting slogan "We Want You," Bryant lists an array of jobs for black youth to consider beyond music, sports, and the military. The number listed in the sections with graceful "helping hands" leads viewers to a supportive hotline, underscoring the value of community in offering guidance and building confidence.

OPPORTUNITY CO$T is a community outreach propaganda campaign that aims to recruit and inform the local youth about the potential careers that await them upon completing high school and/or college. We realize that exposure to different professions and lifestyles play a major role in the development of a person's social experience, future, and their overall well being. It is our mission to bring awareness to underresourced and underappreciated areas for the sole purpose of building self-sufficient communities that thrive on love, innovation and commerce.
DO US A FAVOR AND HELP SPREAD THE WORD

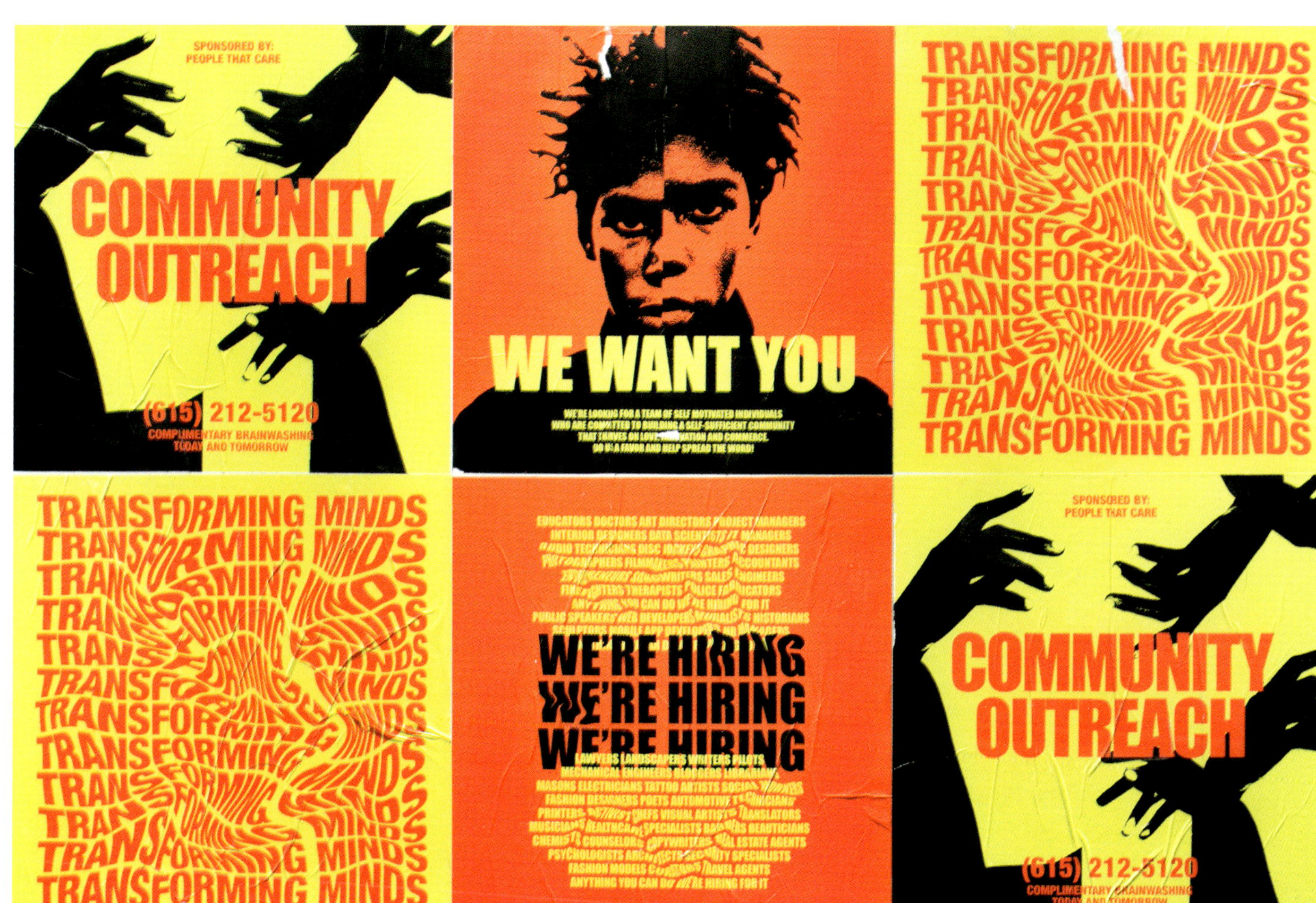

OPPORTUNITY CO$T, 2019
Graphic and wheat paste on panel

OTHER WORK

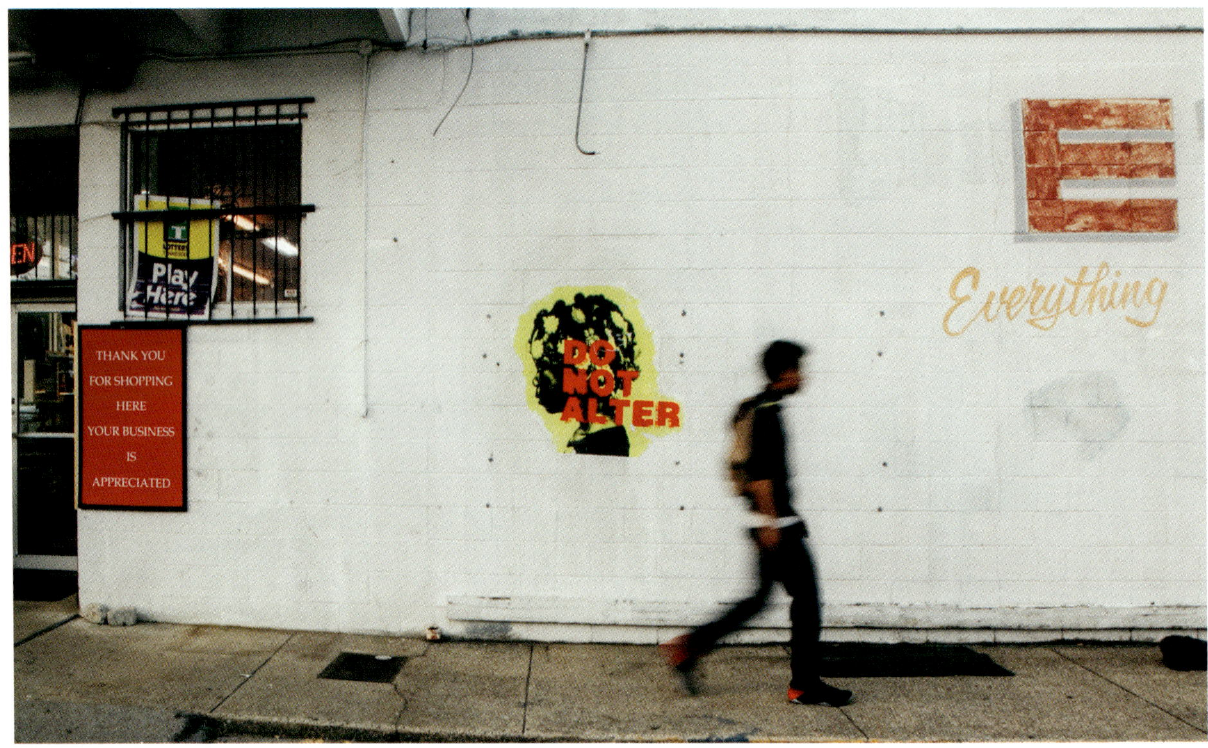

LeXander Bryant. *Do Not Alter*, 2017. Located at 947 28th Avenue North. Created for *Guns and Butter: The Art of Public Manipulation*. Supported by the Metro Arts Learning Lab Program and in part by an award from the National Endowment for the Arts. Photo and artwork © LeXander Bryant

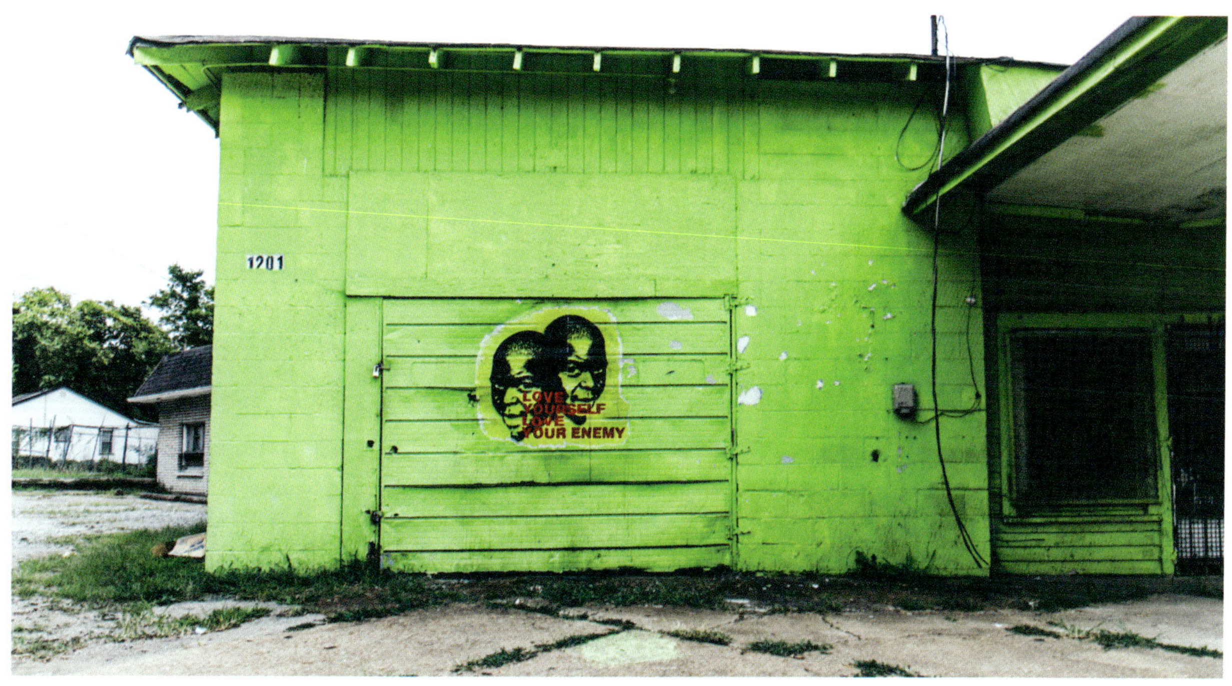

LeXander Bryant. *Love Yourself Love Your Enemy*, 2017. Located at Buchanan and 10th Avenue North. Created for *Guns and Butter: The Art of Public Manipulation*. Supported by the Metro Arts Learning Lab Program and in part by an award from the National Endowment for the Arts. Photo and artwork © LeXander Bryant

XPAYNE

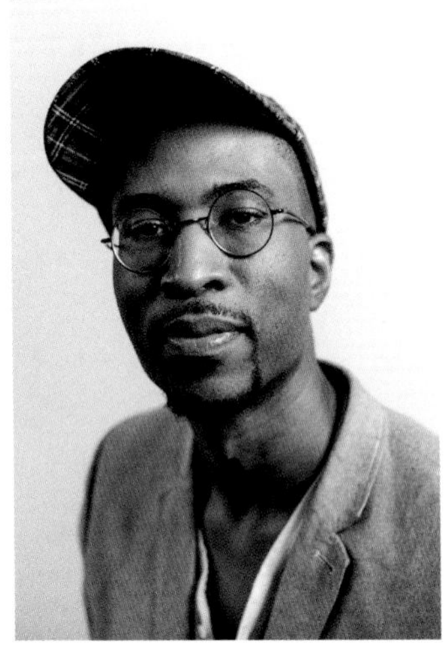

XPayne, a graduate of Watkins College of Art, is a graphic designer and illustrator whose powerful billboard campaign "Don't Tread on Me" blanketed North Nashville in 2017. *Adaptation* also speaks directly to gentrification. The mural features a young superhero being pushed out of his familiar environment, losing his Mickey Mouse ears along the way. When he lands, he is given African weapons from an imposing and strong Batman-like figure, representing the transfer of wisdom from elders to youth. With the spear and shield, and fire burning nearby buildings, the boy fiercely attempts to slay the green dragon of greed. Stickers with a black Rosie the Riveter designed by XPayne punctuate the scene, adding a sense of collective confidence and underscoring the historic nature of this fight for independence and ownership of land.

XPayne refers to his style—the use of bold colors and flat forms to depict African American figures—as "Black Pop," and he adopts this pictorial language as a way to write people that look like him into popular culture. In doing so, he demonstrates that black people often feel and act the same way as white people and shows the significant influence that African Americans have had on popular culture, from Spike Lee movies to hip-hop music.

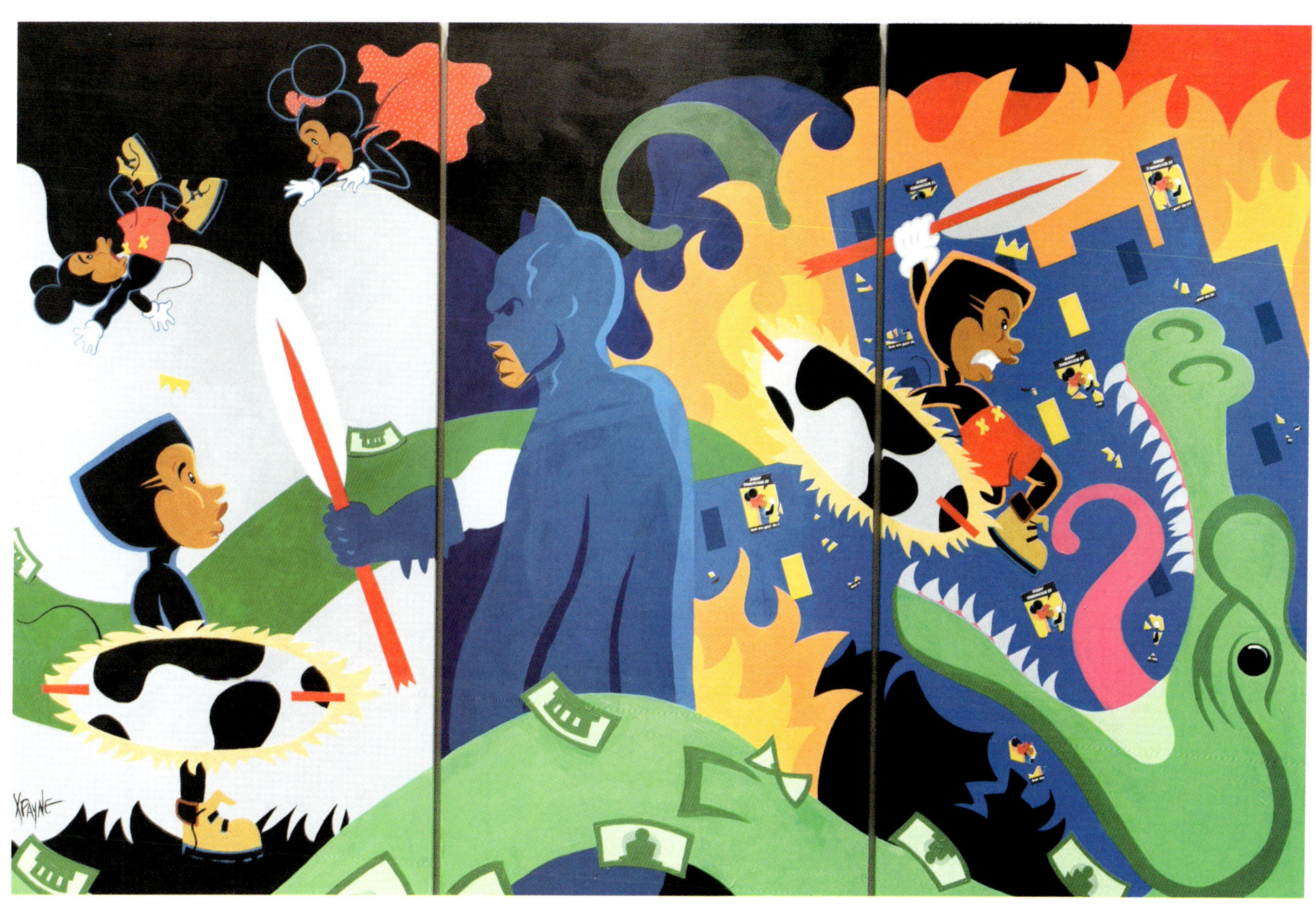

Adaptation, 2019
Acrylic and stickers on panel

OTHER WORK

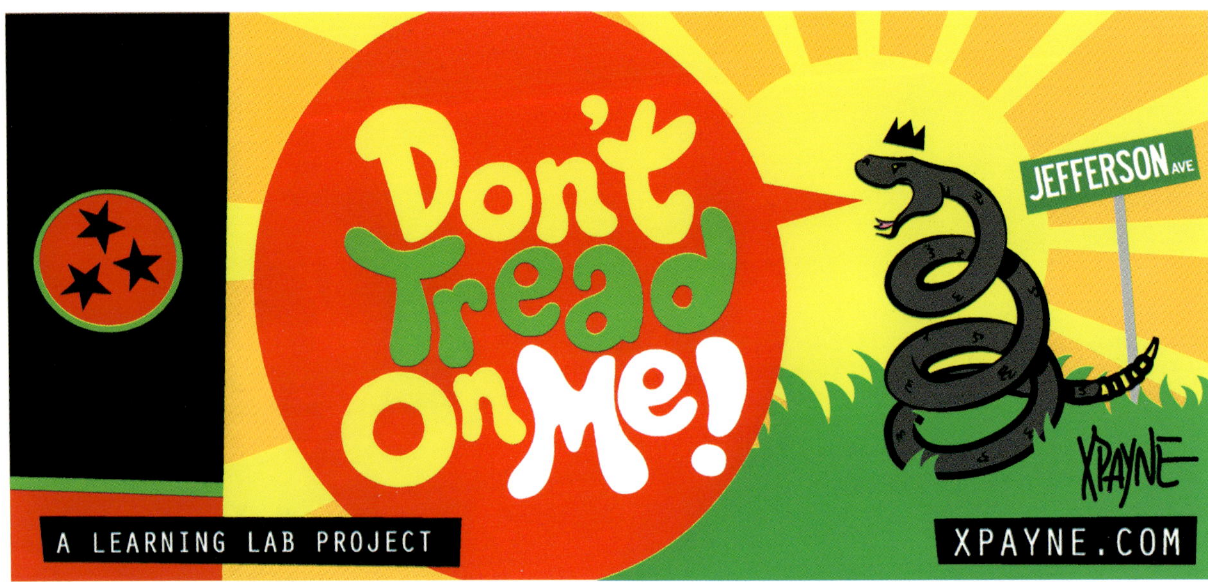

XPayne. *Don't Tread on Me*, 2017. One of six billboards installed along Jefferson Street (now removed). Supported by the Metro Arts Learning Lab Program and in part by an award from the National Endowment for the Arts. © XPayne

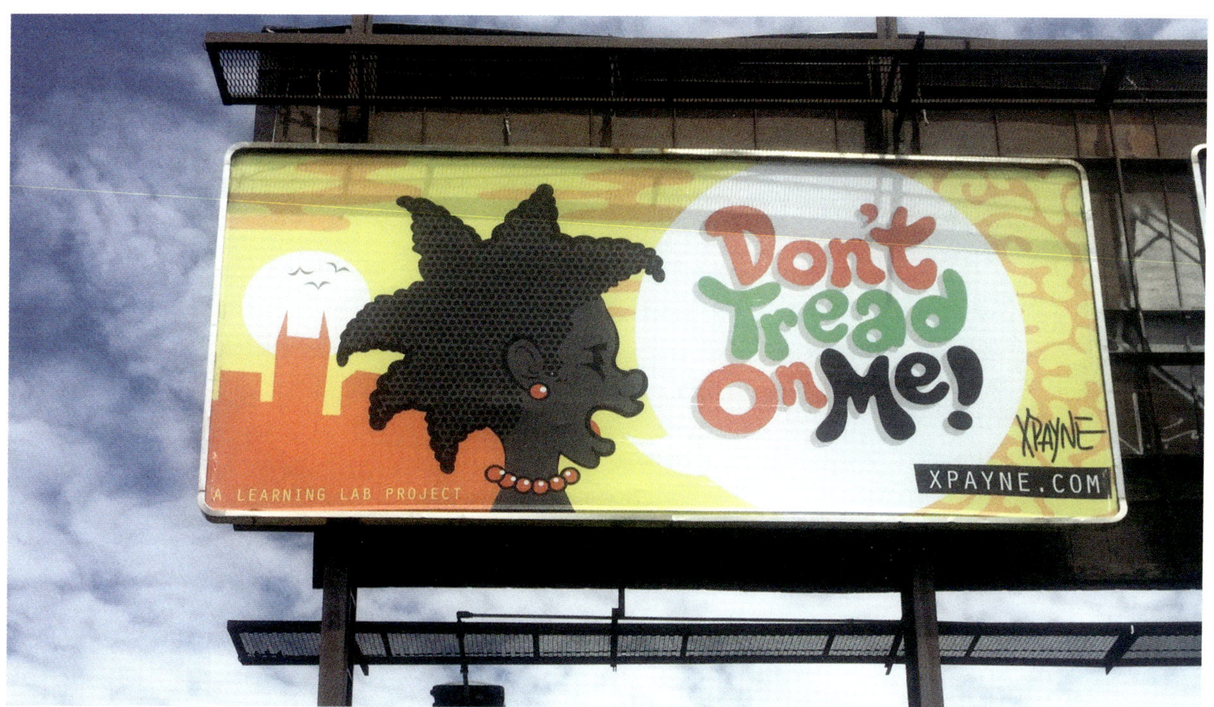

XPayne. *Don't Tread on Me*, 2017. One of six billboards installed along Jefferson Street (now removed). Supported by the Metro Arts Learning Lab Program and in part by an award from the National Endowment for the Arts. Photo and artwork © XPayne

BRANDON DONAHUE

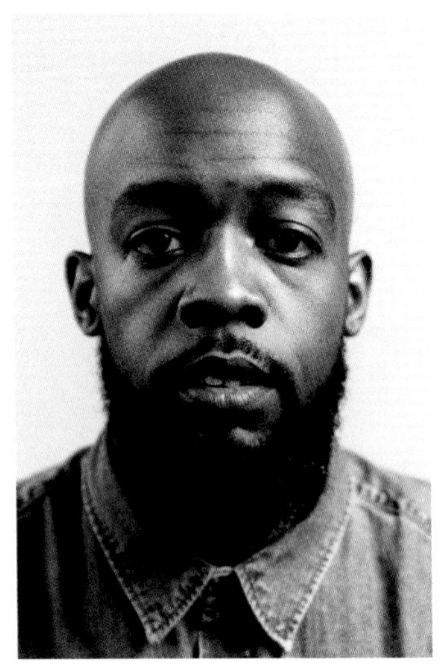

Brandon Donahue created this memorial wall, similar in concept to Maya Lin's Vietnam Veterans Memorial, to commemorate local victims of homicide. Using information gathered by *Tennessean* reporter Natalie Neysa Alund, he carefully airbrushed the names of ninety-six murdered Nashvillians: eighty-five in 2018 and eleven in early 2019. Over 85 percent died from gunshot wounds. The deceased include five- and eight-year-old sisters Samaii and Sammarree Daniel, who were killed in their front yard in the Cumberland Gardens neighborhood; Jaime Sarrantonio and Bartley Teal, who were robbed and shot at a bar in East Nashville; Daniel Hambrick, who was killed by a police officer in North Nashville; and Akilah Dasilva, DeEbony Groves, Joe R. Perez, and Taurean Sanderlin, massacred at the Waffle House on Murfreesboro Pike. Some of these deaths were reported extensively in the media, while others received very little attention.

Donahue, a graduate of and professor at Tennessee State University, worked in a T-shirt shop and wrote graffiti as a youth in Nashville. Honoring each victim through very individualized airbrushing brings a sense of gravitas to imagery that one might associate with tourist souvenirs without knowing the context. This elevation of everyday items and popular culture into a gallery context is also a part of Donahue's studio practice.

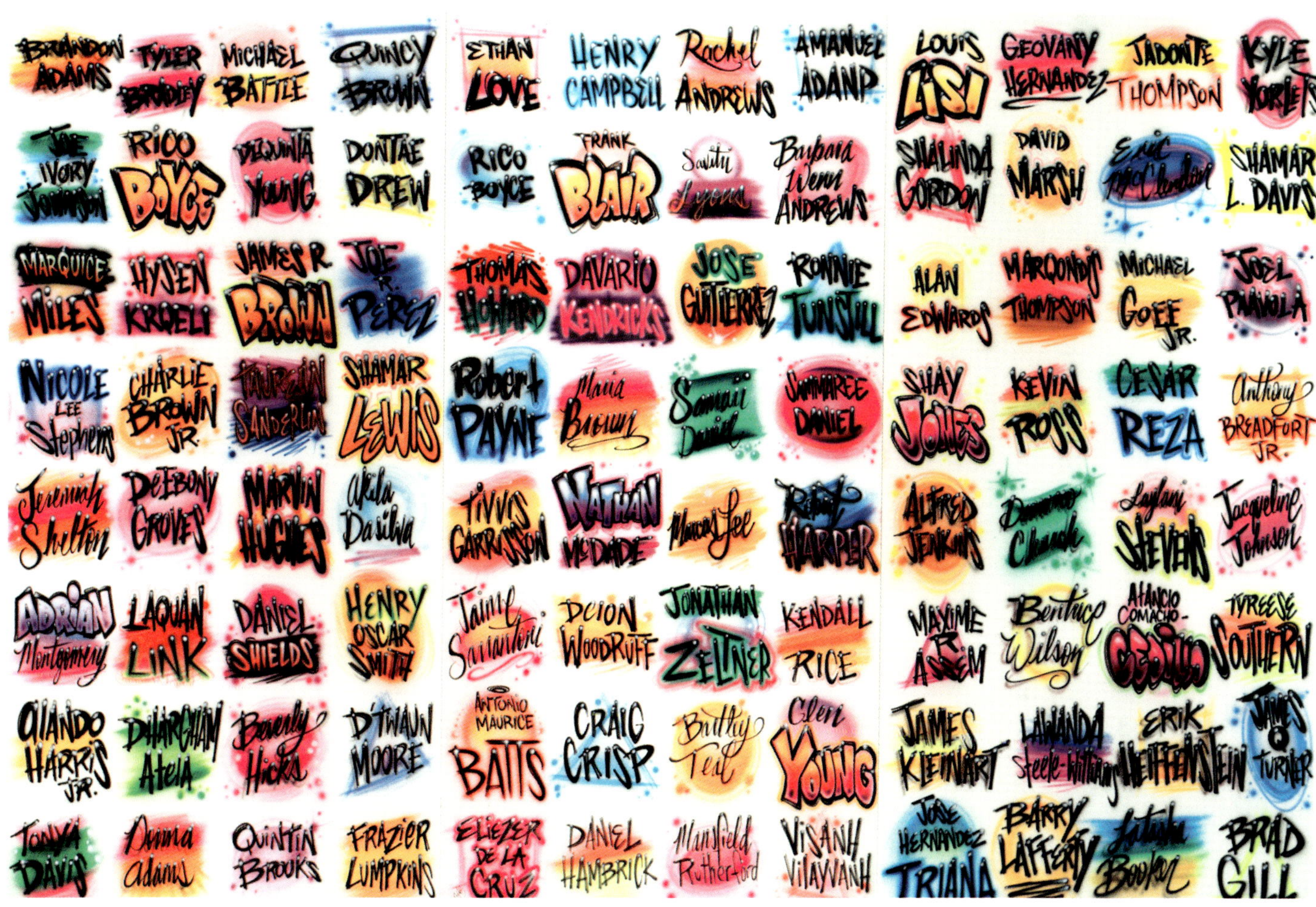

Rest in Peace, 2019
Airbrush acrylic on panel

OTHER WORK

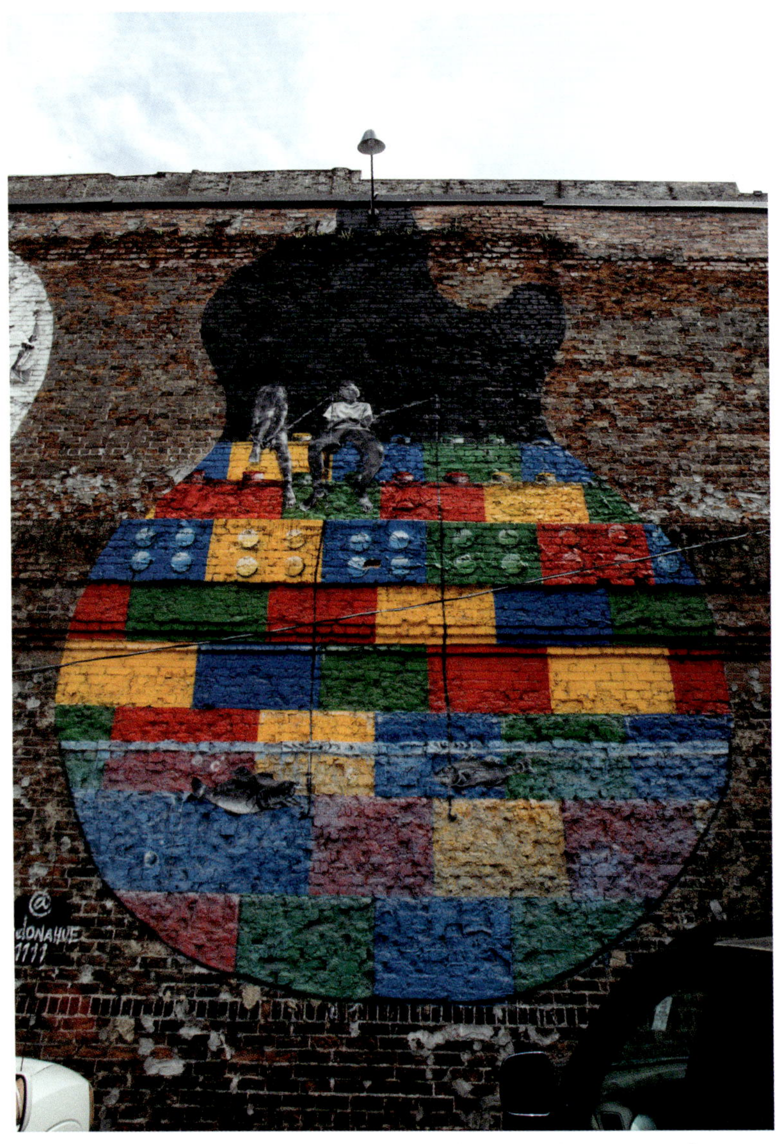

Brandon Donahue. *Gone Fishin'*, 2016. Located at 213 3rd Avenue North. Created for the Nashville Walls Project Gibson Tribute Mural. Sponsored by Gibson Custom Division and FirstBank. © Brandon Donahue. Photo: keep3

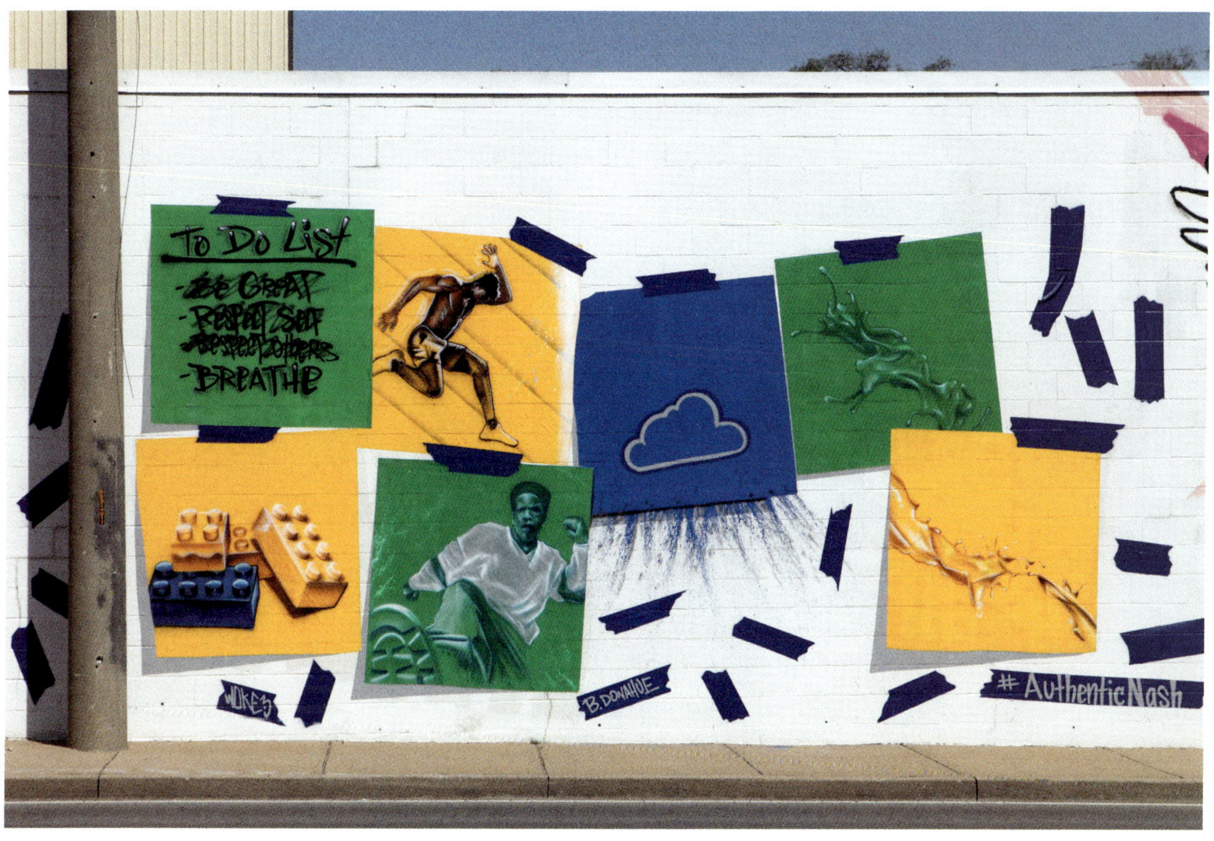

Brandon Donahue. *Sprite Mural*, 2018. Located at 3020 Charlotte Avenue. Created for Off the Wall Nashville. Sponsored by Coca-Cola Consolidated. © Brandon Donahue. Photo: Blu Sanders

OMARI BOOKER

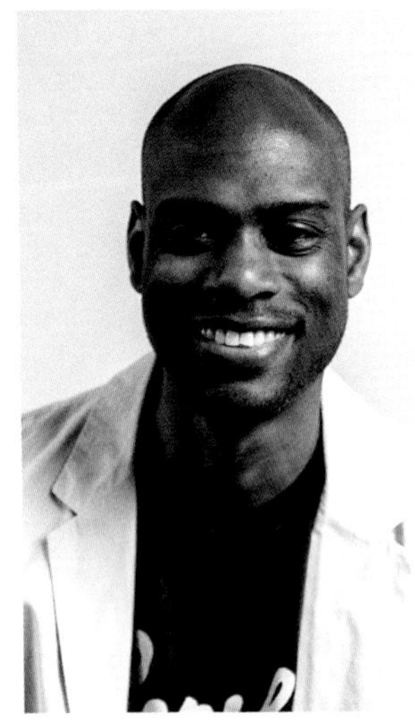

A 2014 graduate of Tennessee State University and longtime employee at Woodcuts Gallery & Framing, Omari Booker has witnessed the physical transformation of North Nashville during the city's current period of growth and development. His mural features the home of Elois Freeman on the 2500 block of Jefferson Street, a house that has been in the family for nearly one hundred years. HomeGuard Housewrap represents the many "tall and skinny" houses currently being constructed throughout the city, including in North Nashville. A small white dog wearing a pink sweater suggests the new residents moving into the neighborhood.

This isn't the first time the Freeman home has been impacted by construction. In the late 1960s, the front yard was lost during the building of Interstate 40. Despite appeals that went all the way to the Supreme Court, hundreds of other houses and businesses along Jefferson were completely destroyed. Through his use of red razor wire to outline Mrs. Freeman's home, Booker also draws attention to the discriminatory lending and investment policies known collectively as "redlining" adopted by banks and the Federal Housing Administration for decades. The legacy of this unfair practice is still felt in the community, where homeownership by residents is far lower than the nation's average.

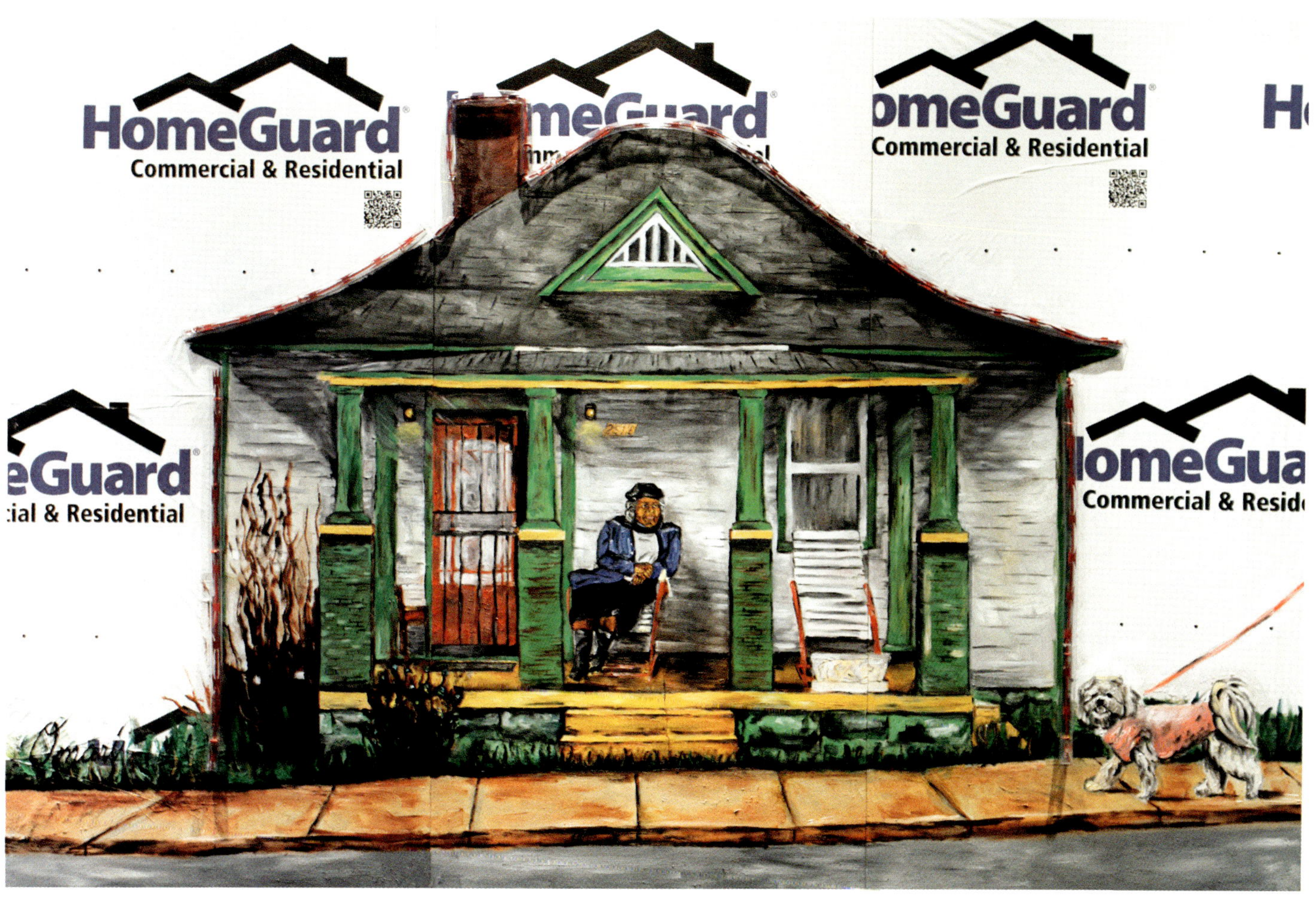

The Writing's on the Walls, 2019
Housewrap, oil, plastic tubing, razor wire, and sand on panel

OTHER WORK

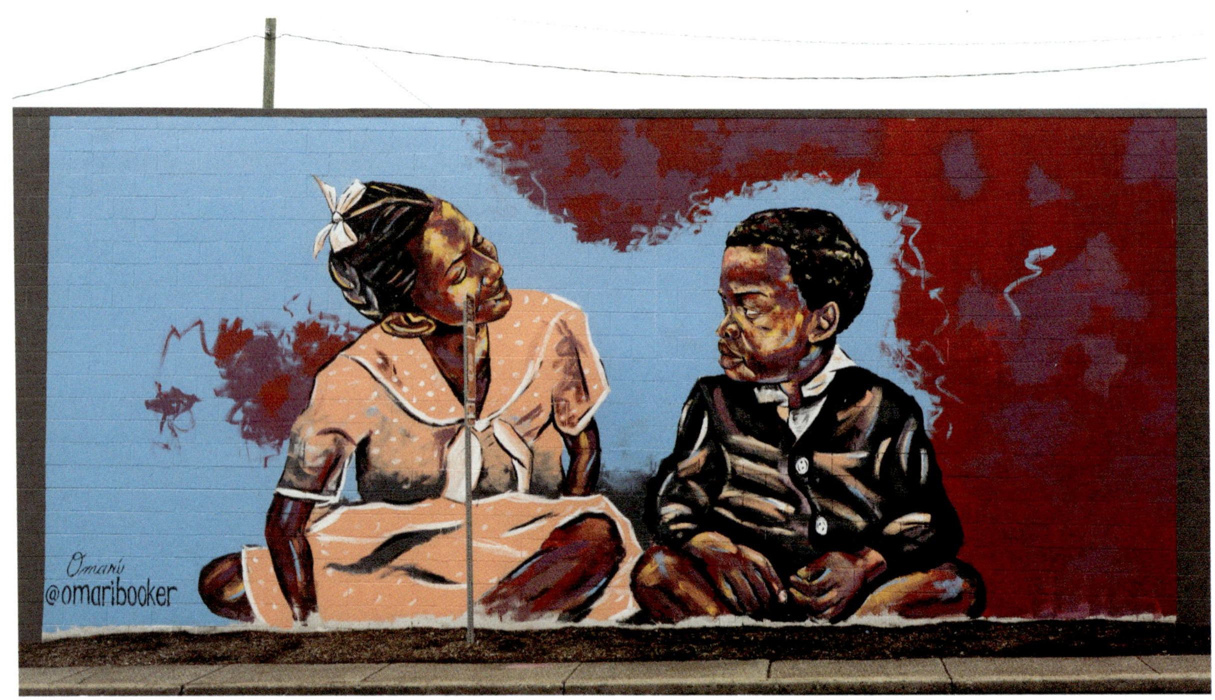

Omari Booker. *You Must Love Me*, 2018. Located at 3020 Charlotte Avenue. Created for Off the Wall Nashville. Sponsored by Buckingham Foundation. © Omari Booker. Photo: Blu Sanders

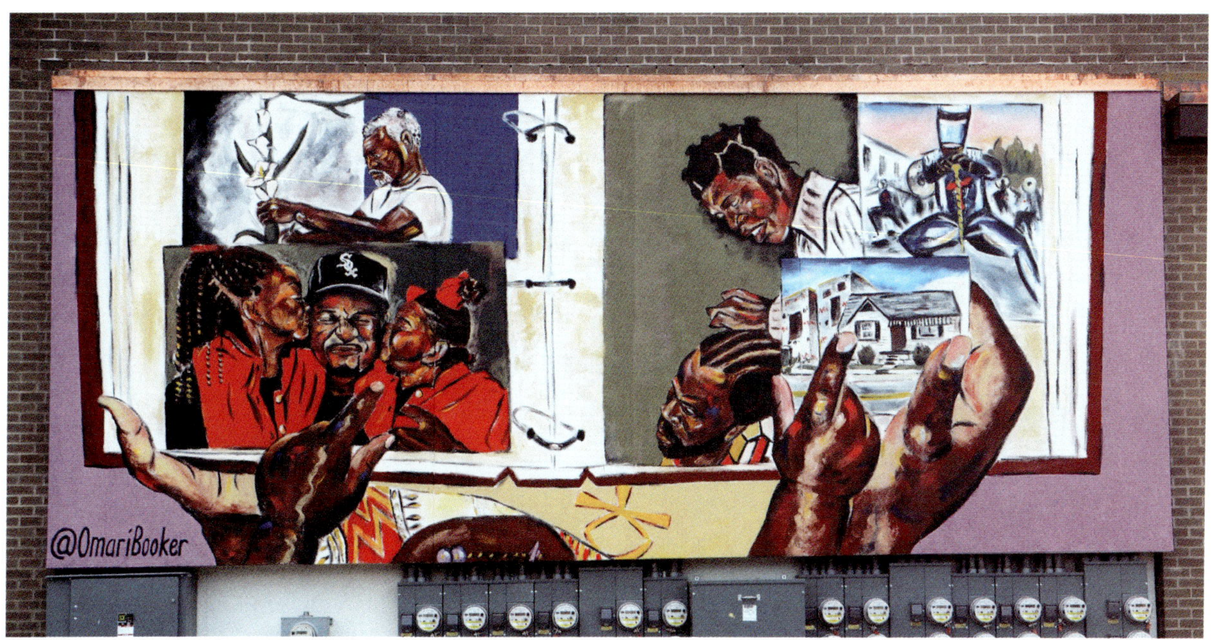

Omari Booker. *I Live Here*, 2019. Located at Clarksville Pike and 26th Avenue North. Completed in partnership with Urban Housing Solutions. © Omari Booker. Photo: Wallace Joiner

NUVEEN BARWARI, MARLOS E'VAN, AND COURTNEY ADAIR JOHNSON

WITH JESUA AGUILAR, SAIRA AGUILAR, KAM'RON ALLEN, ASEEL ALSABIL, MELODI LEIVA ARREOLA, ASHANTI CHATMAN, ISAIAH M. CROUCH, NADIA CRUZ, KIMORA CUNNINGHAM, NEVAEH FLOWERS, AF'REKA HOLLOWAY, JOY IBRAHIM, MAXIMOS IBRAHIM, MAKYIA L. LACY, MAINER MALDENADO, RANDY MANCIA, ANGEL MCELRATH, ARYAN PHUYAL, AND SAMARI LASHA SIMS

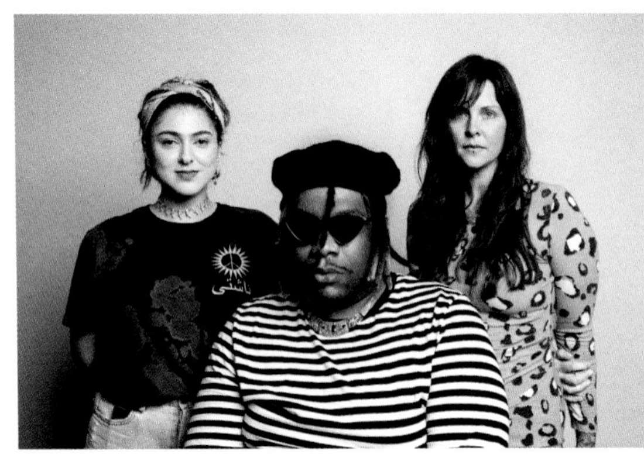

Youth enrolled in the Opportunity NOW internship program at the McGruder Social Practice Artist Residency (M-SPAR) were asked to mentor participants from the International Teen Outreach Program (ITOP) hosted by the Oasis Center. Both groups met with teaching artists Courtney Adair Johnson, Marlos E'van, and Nuveen Barwari and, with M-SPAR's guidance, were able to reflect artistically on their heritage in connection to current social topics. As one example, the materials used on this mural are from sustainably sourced and reused items as a part of M-SPAR's mission to make art with low to no waste.

The young artists toured and documented several of North Nashville's cultural venues, including Jefferson Street Sound, Fisk University's Carl Van Vechten Gallery, and murals from the 2015 Norf Wall Fest. Afterward, the youth shared their ideas and began to organize their research into themes of past, present, and hopes for the future. Each panel on display represents a separate time period, embedded with the creators' observations.

As the young participants created the mural together, some brainstormed concepts while others illustrated those ideas on the panels. They frequently stated that everyone wants to live in a healthy world where all people have access to basic needs and rights, as Nashvillians and as global citizens.

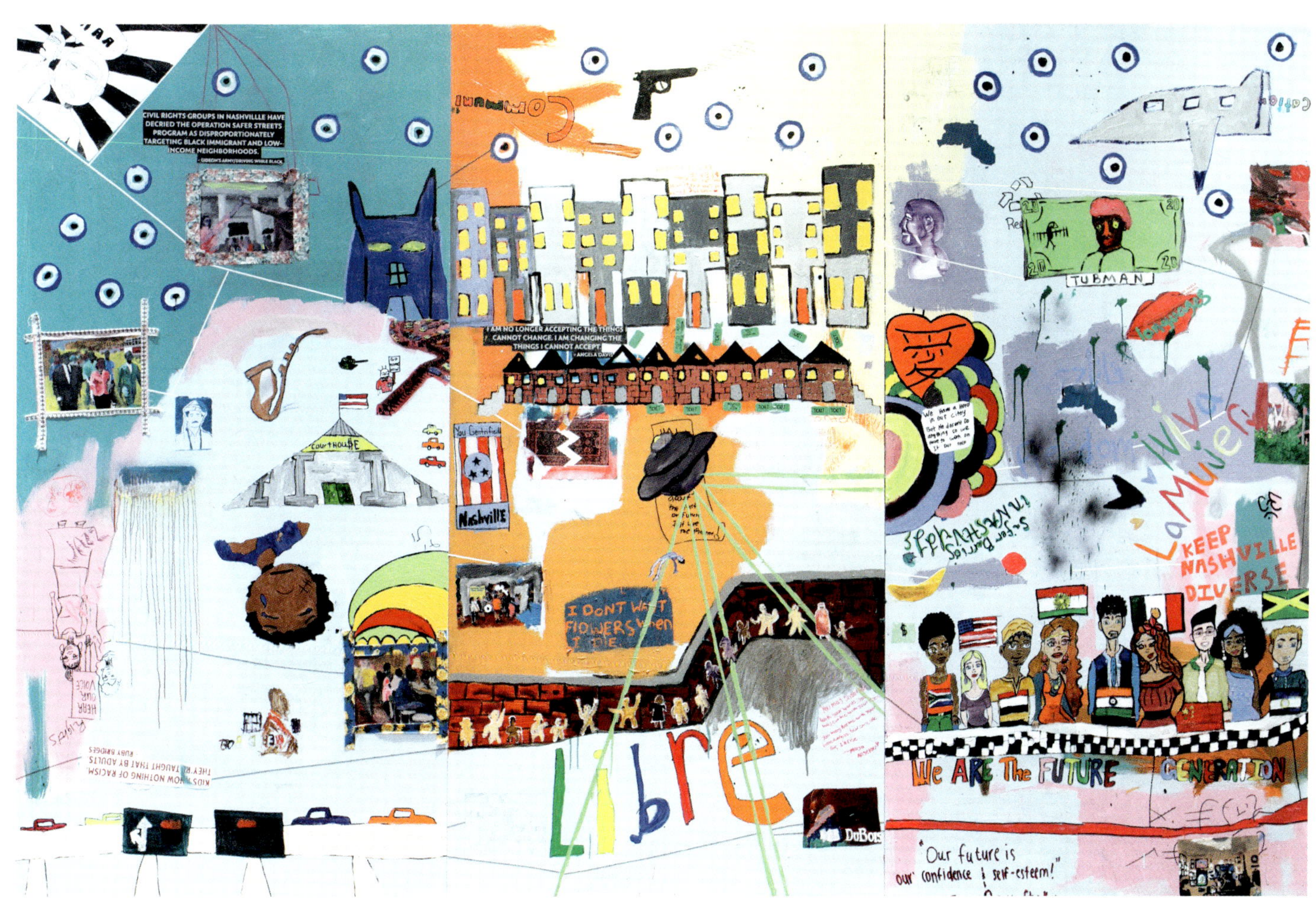

Where we were. Where we are. Where we are going. 2019
Mixed media on panel

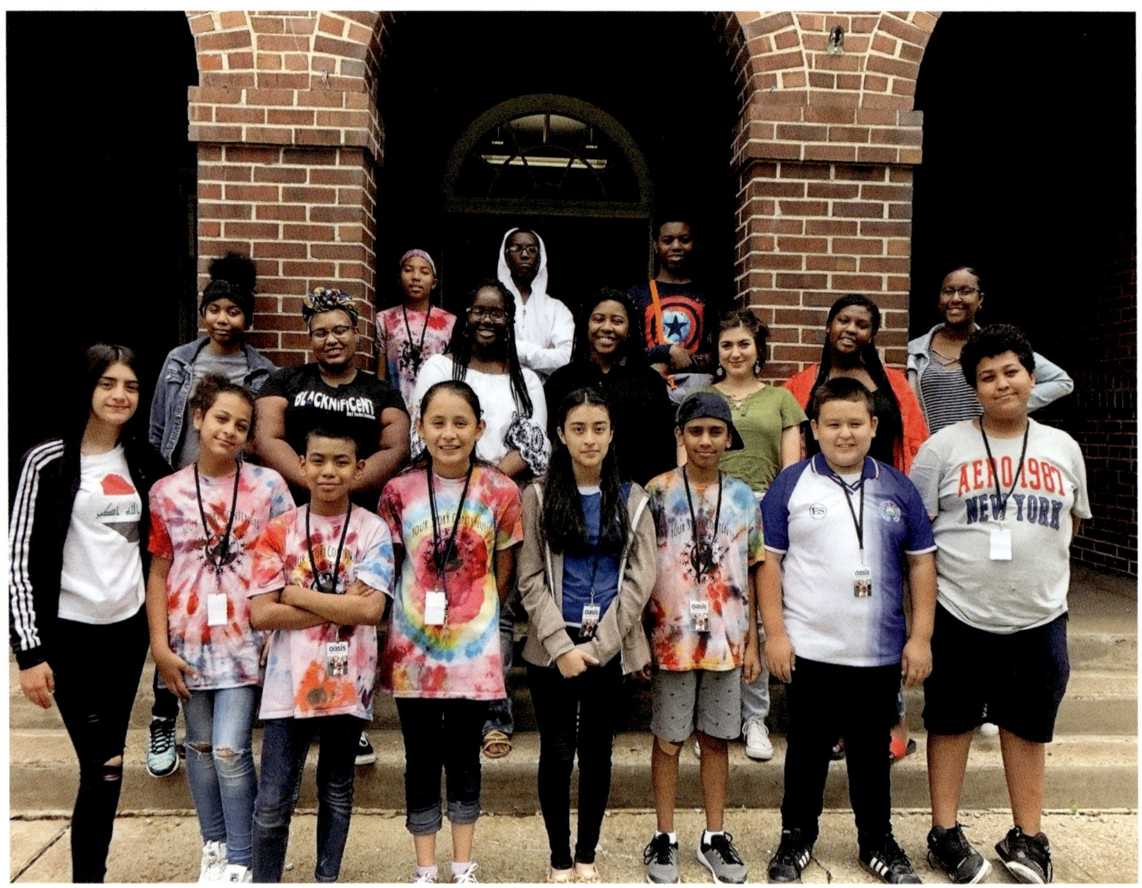

Photo: Michayla George

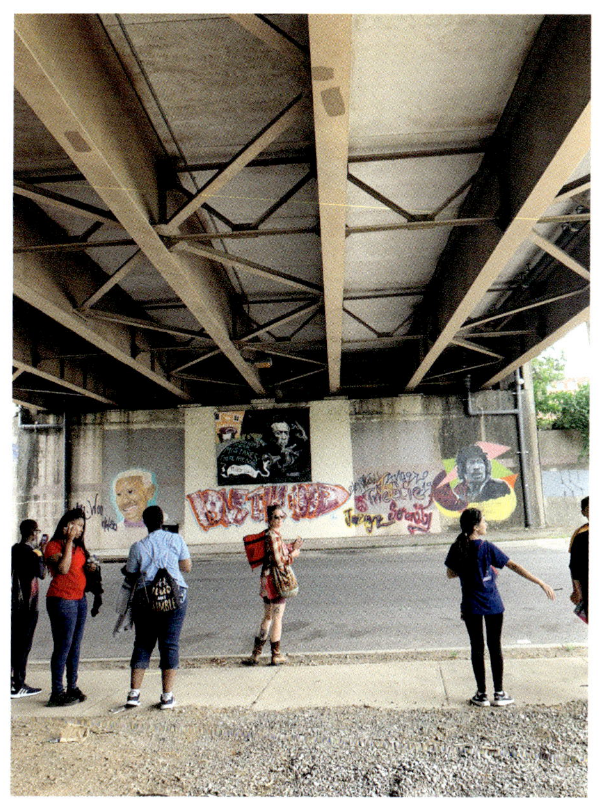

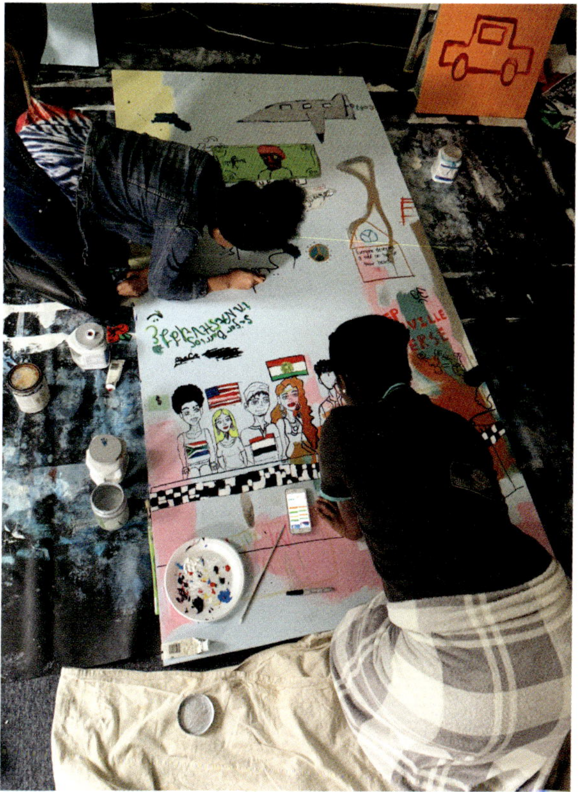

Photos: Rosemary Brunton

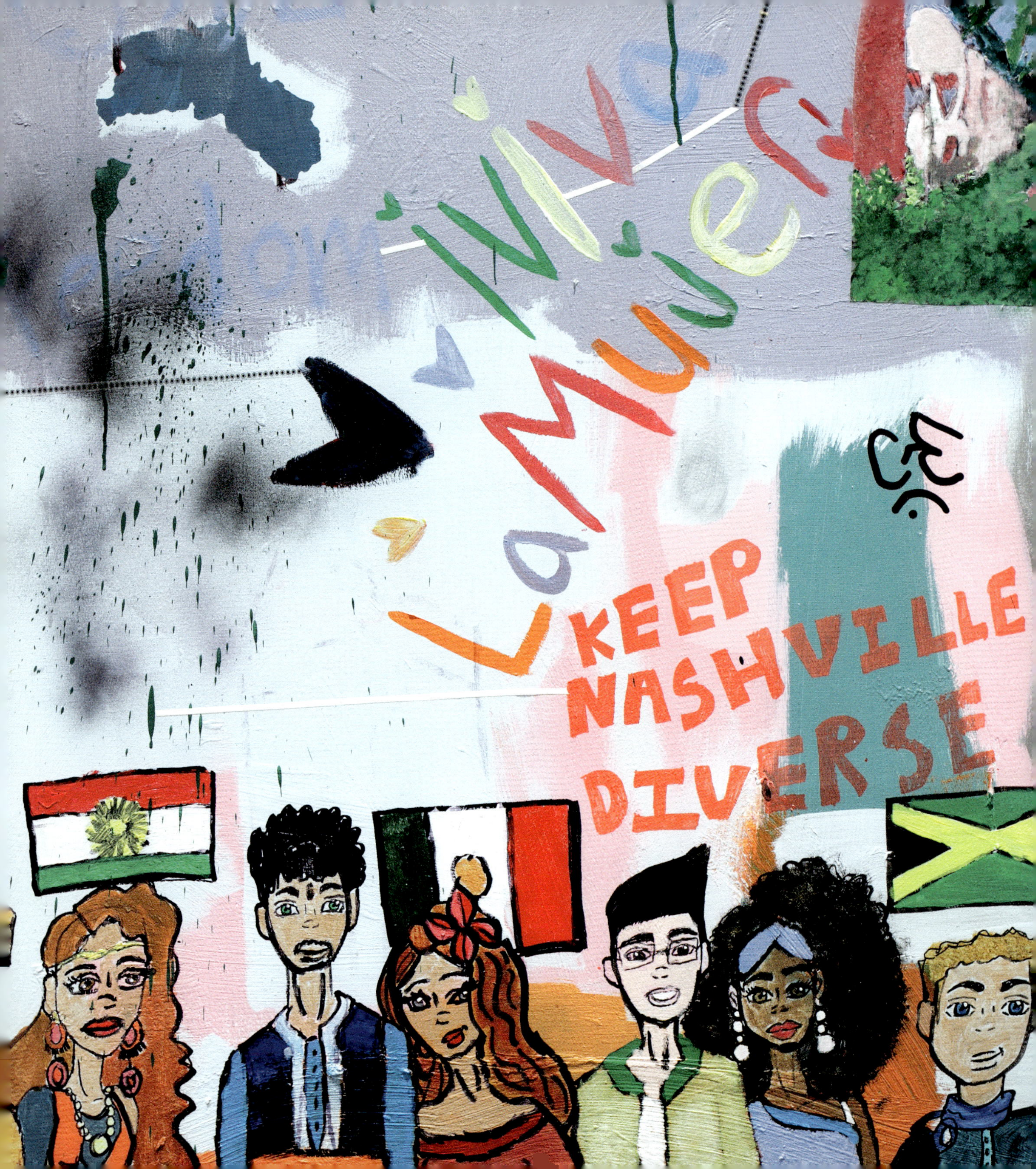
¡Viva La Mujer!
KEEP NASHVILLE DIVERSE

CONTRIBUTORS

Kathryn E. Delmez is curator at the Frist Art Museum

Dr. Susan H. Edwards is executive director and CEO of the Frist Art Museum

Dr. Learotha Williams Jr. is associate professor of African American and public history at Tennessee State University and coordinator of the North Nashville Heritage Project